When a dim sum cart packed
with delicious, fragrant goodies
rolls past your table, it's hard to resist
the sweet, salty crunch of *char siu* pork, or
the juicy flavor explosion of a steamed dumpling.
But these classics are only a sliver of what the
world of dim sum has to offer. So the next time
you're brunching with friends, bring along the
The Dim Sum Field Guide, which has profiles and
illustrations of more than 70 dim sum delicacies,
from buns to beignets, chicken feet to crab
claws. Soon, you'll be ordering—and
eating!—like a pro.

THE DIM SUM FIELD GUIDE

Written and Illustrated by
CAROLYN PHILLIPS

THE
DIM SUM
FIELD GUIDE

粵式點心譜

A Taxonomy of Dumplings, Buns, Meats, Sweets,
and Other Specialties of the Chinese Teahouse

TEN SPEED PRESS
BERKELEY

CONTENTS

INTRODUCTION

Welcome to the delicious world of dim sum. This is an exquisitely leisurely way to brunch, a meal that, when done right, can easily stretch out for a couple of hours into the afternoon. Each one- or two-bite morsel of dim sum is essentially a small packet of unique flavors—just enough to grab your attention and whet the appetite—but small enough that you can move on to the next tantalizing dish before your palate becomes bored.

This book explores the Cantonese form of dim sum, which was born in the teahouses of Southern China—specifically, the capital city of Guangzhou that straddles the great Pearl River—about two centuries ago. Of course, the history of dim sum stretches back much farther than that (*jiaozi*-like dumplings, for example, were discovered in a Tang dynasty tomb dating from thirteen hundred years ago), and many other parts of the country boast of wonderful arrays of teatime snacks and petite sweets. However, I would have to agree with those who claim that the culinary art form known as dim sum reached its absolute pinnacle in Guangzhou.

Perhaps the secret lies in the land. Located on the lush, fertile plains of southern Guangdong, this area has an almost endless selection of vegetables, starches, fruits, animals, crustaceans, and seafood. Or maybe it's the people, for Guangdong has been the destination for immigrants from all over the country who longed for more peaceful lives and who made Guangzhou synonymous with gracious living. Or maybe it's the tropical weather, the type of climate that encourages a person to laze in the shade with a hot pot of tea and some savory snacks, a trickle of water and the rattle of bamboo leaves in the warm wind coming together to form a natural lullaby. Or maybe it is because Guangzhou was a nexus between East and West, as well as North and South, a place where foreign culinary inspiration gave birth to marvelous ideas in the kitchen, while imperial and Muslim tastes added their own rich notes to this culinary symphony. Or maybe it is because all of these great food traditions eventually made their way down the Pearl River to Hong Kong, where ancient history crashed into the modern world, and many dim sum dishes evolved into their delicious, present-day incarnations.

Whatever the reasons, dim sum remains one of the most delightful ways ever invented for whiling away a few hours in the middle of the day. And despite what some think, dim sum is a whole lot more than "dumplings," a sort of catchall English term for anything vaguely starchy and small in the dim sum brigade. There's nothing inherently wrong, of course, with calling these dumplings, but it's sort of like labeling scarlet, chartreuse, and bronze simply "colors," when they are so much more thrilling than that. The fact is that dim sum covers an intense spectrum of flavors, aromas, textures, and ingredients, and they are very much worth getting to know on a personal basis.

Which is where *The Dim Sum Field Guide* fits in. My hope is that this book will inspire you to explore the many offerings in dim sum teahouses, whether you carry it with you on your next field excursion, or simply flip through it at home. If dim sum ends up giving you even half the pleasure it has handed to me, I know you will be a dedicated fan for the rest of your life.

A BRIEF HISTORY OF DIM SUM

"Dim sum" is the Cantonese pronunciation of 點心 • *diǎnxīn*, a verb that a thousand years ago merely meant "to eat a little something." It was not until somewhere around the year 1300 that *diǎnxīn* evolved into a noun meaning "snacks" or "very light meals," a definition that has more or less remained unchanged to this day.

Dim sum probably had their earliest origins as tea snacks in the north around one thousand years ago, but it took another five centuries before Southern China—and particularly Guangdong—was reveling in its very own versions. Nearly every area of China has iconic snack traditions; however, the demarcation between North and South in almost all discussion of China's foods has been (and probably always will be) the Yangtze River because the climate, ingredients, geography, aesthetics, languages, and cultures of the two halves are just so very different.

What this means when it comes to food is that Northern China has traditionally reveled in the heartier, wheat-based snacks of the ethnic Muslims there (known to the Chinese as the Hui people), such as the stuffed buns called *baozi* (page 20) and the ravioli-like *jiaozi* (page 14). These were designed to satisfy hungry people in cold climates, while a battery of quivering jellies (page 150) were handed down to us as culinary heirlooms from the imperial kitchens of Beijing's Forbidden City. In the warm lands along the Pearl River, though, rice dough and tropical ingredients such as taro and coconut pop up just as much in the local dim sum as wheat.

Guangdong's most famous dim sum most likely evolved from the sophisticated treats served in elegant salons along the Yangtze and were greatly influenced by dishes that wound their way south from the capital in Changan (today's Xi'an) in the North, which might explain the presence of pot stickers (page 16) and many other pasta or raised wheat dough dishes in the Cantonese dim sum repertoire. Add to that the increased contact and trade with the West a couple of hundred years ago, which led to foreign touches like custard and curry, and suddenly the cultural and historical tendrils that shaped this scintillating branch of Cantonese cuisine make a whole lot of sense.

HOW TO USE THIS GUIDE

Dining on dim sum is easy once you get the basics down pat. And this book is going to help you do that.

First, keep in mind that the names of these dishes—especially the English ones—will vary widely from place to place once you get out into the real world. For example, you might find Siu Mai (page 18) called "shrimp and pork dumplings" or *shui mai* or *shiu mai* or *sui mai* or *shao mai* or some other combination of these words, because some people have just winged it over the years when it came to transposing Chinese pronunciations into English. That is one of the reasons why we have so many illustrations in this book, as well as the name of each dish in Mandarin, Cantonese, and traditional Chinese characters. And so, the easiest way to get what you want the first couple of times you eat at a dim sum teahouse is to simply point at the *siu mai*, either in this book or on one of the carts that are wheeled around the room.

Second, each restaurant will have its own recipes, or at least it should. One place we frequent has a special way with Braised Duck Chins (page 62), for example, as they add unbelievable layers of texture and flavor to the dish, and it has become my gold standard for that particular recipe. What this also means is that the ingredients for each item will most likely vary to some degree, so if you have any food allergies, be sure to quiz the restaurant on what is in each dish.

Third, be adventurous. Try at least one new dish each time you dine. Blanched Goose Intestines (page 64), for example, might not sound at all appetizing in English, no matter how you spin the translation. But contrary to what your mind will be screaming at you—warning that this is something that you most definitely do not want near your mouth—you might very well end up being permanently charmed by these fluttery pieces of edible silk, which are delectable when an experienced chef is at the helm. The Chinese have had thousands of years to get things right in their food world, so it's always best to leap into these dishes with an open mind and a very wide mouth.

Think of *The Dim Sum Field Guide* as your road map on this gustatory trip. The drawings will let you know what to expect from each order—whether it's served in a steamer, on a plate, or in a bowl—and how many pieces usually appear per serving. Underneath the name of the dish are little symbols that tell you very quickly what to expect from this dish—Is there pork in there, or shellfish? Should you special order it? Is it supposed to be served hot? Can a vegetarian possibly eat it?—as all of these things are set out clearly in the key on page 11.

The right-hand page for each entry then goes into even greater detail: what the dish's textures and flavors should be, some background information on how it came into being, what variations you might expect to find, and more.

FEASTING IN A DIM SUM TEAHOUSE

One of the greatest pleasures of eating dim sum is the opportunity to leisurely check out all of the carts passing by your table, many filled with foods you might have never even heard of before. As they wheel along, mere inches from your nose, you may be tempted to start ordering every dish you see. While that might initially seem like a great idea, you run the risk of an overcrowded table and an underplanned meal. So, one of the greatest challenges of eating at a dim sum teahouse is figuring out what to order so that you are not overwhelmed.

In dim sum teahouses, each cart tends to offer a specific type of dish. For example, one might be dedicated to small steamers of *siu mai* and *char siu* buns, another one will have plates with roast meats, another will have fried sweets, another will have soupy savory dishes, and so forth. You can always flag one of the cart-wielding servers down and peruse his or her (although it's most often her) offerings. As she stops by your table, ask her to open up steamers for you and tell you what's inside. You can always point to things in this book to help things along if there's a language barrier.

Ordering

The absolute first thing you will be asked by your waiter is what type of tea you want to drink. Prepare for this by reading "Tea Varietals" (page 7) and discussing this with your fellow diners so that you can immediately answer on behalf of your table. A large teapot full of fresh tea will then appear. Let it steep for around five minutes and then pour out tea for everyone. Place the teapot near the center of the table or on the lazy Susan so all the diners can reach it; or, you can keep it near you if you want to be extra polite and serve folks—it's all up to you.

If you are in charge of figuring out the meal, then read through the list on the dim sum–specific menu (often printed on a sheet of paper that you can mark up with a pencil). Decide how many of each dish you'd like and write the quantity (like "1" or "2") next to the dim sum you want. Most dim sum will have three or four pieces, and these can sometimes be cut in half by your server. Count on at least one dish per person to start, so that if you have five people at your table, order around five things for the first round. Starving diners can always flag down a cart for immediate satiation of their hunger pangs, and I often try to have one or two things placed on the table right away in order to get the meal off to a happy start.

As the waitstaff set dishes in front of you, they will stamp either a Chinese printout of your order or a tally divided into sections according to price (generally categorized as small, medium, and large plates, but which may include things like special orders); be sure and keep this near the edge of the table where they serve the dishes. Printouts are provided when you have asked for things from your waiter and are having foods sent to you directly from the kitchen, while the tally is used mainly to keep track of the items you select from the carts. Once the meal is over, everything is totted up, including the charge for tea, which is calculated per person. Be sure to add a tip when you pay.

Paying the Bill

If you are dining with Chinese friends, expect to fight over the check, even if everyone agreed that you or they were hosting the meal. This is just good manners—please do lunge at the check when it arrives; it is also considered very gracious and clever to preempt this friendly tussle by secretly paying the cashier while ostensibly visiting the restroom. Whoever gets the check should feel triumphant and pay with pleasure while the others protest vociferously, as this gives the host great face. If you are so lucky as to treat everyone, brush off these protests by saying, "*Xiàcì, xiàcì*" ("next time, next time").

And so, when you are ready to settle up with the teahouse, raise your hand to get the waitstaff's attention and ask for the check in English or Chinese (買單 · *mǎidān* · *maai⁵ daan¹*). Your orders and the checklist on your table will be tallied at the front counter, while someone else arranges to have the leftovers boxed up.

TEA VARIETALS

As noted earlier, you will have to choose the type of tea you want placed on your table before anything else, so now is the time to figure out what's what. All of these teas go well with dim sum, so selecting the right one really comes down to personal taste.

GREEN TEA · 綠茶 · *lǜchá* · *luk⁶ caa⁴*
This is the lightest of teas. It has a very pale green brew that smells of fresh-mown grass and is relatively low in caffeine.

OOLONG TEA · 烏龍茶 · *wūlóngchá* · *wu¹ lung⁴ caa⁴*
The natural floral notes of this semifermented varietal set it apart from all others. It has a golden brew with a wonderful fragrance. The fresh leaves are bruised to release their juices and then left to slightly ferment before being dried.

BLACK TEA · 紅茶 · *hóngchá* · *hung⁴ caa⁴*
The deep mahogany of this brew is what led to its Chinese name, which means "red tea." (The English name comes from the color of the dried leaves.) A fruity edge to this much-stronger tea shows that it has been fully fermented.

PU'ER (OR PU-ERH) TEA · 普洱茶 · *pǔěrchá* · *pou² ji⁵ caa⁴*
The fully fermented form of this compressed tea is the darkest of all Chinese brews. Made mainly in Yunnan province, the leaves are usually bruised and oxidized (not naturally like other teas, but with things like bacteria and fungus), and that gives this unique tea its pleasant, earthy taste with a gently sweet edge. The leaves are formed into disks or bricks for easier transport.

CHRYSANTHEMUM TEA · 菊花茶 · *júhuāchá* · *guk¹ faa¹ caa⁴*
No tea leaves are used here, just dried tiny yellow chrysanthemums, which means that this golden brew is caffeine free.

CHRYSANTHEMUM PU'ER · 菊普 · *júpǔ* · *guk¹ pou²*
A personal favorite, this tea combines the floral headiness of the chrysanthemums with the earthy tones of *pu'er* tea leaves, which results in a deeply hued brew that spans a wide range of flavors and aromas.

JASMINE TEA · 花茶 · *huāchá* · *faa¹ caa⁴*
Simply referred to as "flower tea" in Chinese, this is green tea with Arabian jasmine blossoms mixed in. As you probably can guess, this pale green brew has a decidedly floral perfume.

LYCHEE (OR LITCHI) TEA · 荔枝茶 · *lìzhīchá* · *lai⁶ zi¹ caa⁴*

Not every teahouse will offer this, but it is a delightful choice if you can get it. This black tea is scented with dried lychees, which makes it the fruitiest of all teas. A dark red brew, this goes well with sweet dim sum.

Whatever tea you decide upon, the pot that is set down upon your table will most likely be filled with loose leaves and boiling hot water. Again, let the tea steep for at least five minutes to allow the flavors and aromas to develop. To check, open up the lid and see whether most of the leaves have settled to the bottom, which means that they have opened up. Then, pour a small amount into your cup and make sure that the color and aroma are correct. At that point, fill up everyone else's cup before your own. If you have a lazy Susan on your table, wheel it around so that a cup appears before each diner.

When everyone has a cup, lift up yours as the host and say, "*Lái lái lái*" ("come, come, come"), which is a signal that you all should toast each other as a sign of welcome. Fill up the teacups as they become half empty, and thank anyone who tops off your cup. (Some people rap the table with their knuckles as a sign of thanks, but others might consider that déclassé.) As the pot becomes empty, set the lid at an angle on the pot—or turn it upside down on the pot if it doesn't want to cooperate—and the waitstaff should automatically refill it with hot water.

If you are enjoying a long, relaxed meal, you may find that the flavor of the tea leaves will peter out before you are done. In that case, ask your waiter to give you a fresh pot. You can even ask for a different type of tea at this point to spice things up. In that case, ask for new teacups, too.

BASIC DINING RULES

As with any food culture, there are a few fundamental bits of dining etiquette that ought to be honored. Here's the rundown:

- Always put the other diners ahead of yourself, whether it comes to serving food or tea.

- Serve yourself only small amounts and finish them before adding more to your plate. At almost any Chinese meal, you may end up having four or five different types of food on your plate, but you're expected to keep them in separate piles and eat them in a tidy manner.

- Remove any bones or shells from your mouth with your chopsticks. Pile them unobtrusively at the edge of your plate; never spit them out or dump them on the tablecloth. If the plates are getting messy, ask the waitstaff to give everyone a new plate.

- Use your chopsticks to eat everything unless your Chinese host uses his or her hands or a spoon; the few exceptions are marked with a "hand" symbol, as with Char Siu Buns (page 20); if you can't use chopsticks, it is perfectly acceptable to ask for a fork.

- Request new plates when you move from the savory dim sum to the sweet ones. Use the serving spoons and/or chopsticks, if they are provided; otherwise, turn your chopsticks upsidedown while serving yourself or others.

- Keep your napkin on the table to your left, rather than on your lap. You may wipe your hands, mouth, and chopsticks with it, but always fold it so that a clean side is on top.

- Rest your nondominant hand on the edge of the table, not on your lap.

- Never stick your chopsticks in your food and leave them there.

- Make sure your chopsticks are clean of food before you remove them from your mouth.

- Signal that you are done eating by placing your chopsticks across the top of your plate, parallel to you.

- As always, fight to pay the bill.

KEY

SPECIAL ORDER	PORK	BONES
CHOPSTICKS + SPOON	NUTS	UNWRAP
HAND	CUT BY SERVER	VEGAN
SHELLFISH	EGGS	CHILES
WHEAT	VEGETARIAN	MILK

SAVORY
DIM SUM

STEAMED JIAOZI

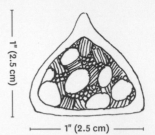

1" (2.5 cm)

1" (2.5 cm)

GENUS 蒸餃 · *zhēngjiǎo* · *zing¹ gaau²*

IDENTIFICATION These pasta packets have a plump gumdrop shape closed with simple folds or multiple pleats across the top. Boiled *jiaozi* are never offered in Cantonese restaurants, as they are exclusively part of Northern cuisines. However, steamed ones have made their way into the teahouse, probably because they fit in so well with the other steamer items on dim sum carts. The best *jiaozi* have jellied stock added, making each mouthful like a hot explosion—an admittedly masochistic pleasure. Exterior is dry and tacky; interior is juicy and meaty. Often called "steamed dumplings" on English menus.

BASIC FILLING
Minced pork plus chopped vegetables such as napa cabbage, bok choy, or garlic chives lightened with diced cellophane noodles.

DEFAULT SAUCE OR DIP
Mix together soy sauce, vinegar, chile oil, and garlic.

NESTING HABITS
These are usually found in groupings of six or more in a medium-size bamboo steamer basket.

ORIGINS
Traditional in the North during Chinese New Year, steamed *jiaozi* most likely traveled south first to the Yangtze River Valley and then finally to Guangzhou, the capital of Guangdong province.

SPECIES
- **Shrimp Steamed Jiaozi**
  鮮蝦蒸餃
  xiānxiā zhēngjiǎo · *sin¹ haa¹ zing¹ gaau²*
  Finely minced fresh shrimp, salt, green onions, and ginger.

- **Garlic Chive Steamed Jiaozi**
  韭菜蒸餃
  jiǔcài zhēngjiǎo · *gau² coi³ zing¹ gaau²*
  Ground pork or scrambled eggs with chopped chives.

- **Pea Sprout Steamed Jiaozi**
  豌豆苗蒸餃
  wāndòumiáo zhengjiǎo · *wun² dau⁶ miu⁴ zing¹ gaau²*
  A Shanghainese favorite with chopped blanched pea sprouts; may contain shrimp or pork.

- **Vegetarian Steamed Jiaozi**
  花素蒸餃
  huāsù zhēngjiǎo · *faa¹ sou³ zing¹ gaau²*
  Finely chopped green vegetables and black mushrooms or wood ear fungus.

POT STICKERS

1" (2.5 cm)

1" (2.5 cm)

GENUS 鍋貼 · *guōtiē* · *wo¹ tip³*

IDENTIFICATION These meat-filled rounds of wheat pasta are crimped all along the top and then steam-fried side-by-side so that they stick gently together in a row. Pot stickers should be served so that the golden bottoms are on top and the packets are still tightly arrayed next to each other. The most traditional forms of pot stickers, such as those made in Tianjin, have a long, even shape and both ends slightly open.

Most teahouse pot stickers are actually Steamed Jiaozi (page 14) that are pan-fried on the bottom, but even so, they can be good if served immediately after they are removed from the stove. Exterior is tacky with a crunchy bottom; interior is juicy and meaty.

BASIC FILLING
Minced pork plus chopped vegetables such as napa cabbage, bok choy, or garlic chives lightened with diced cellophane noodles.

DEFAULT SAUCE OR DIP
Mix together soy sauce, vinegar, chile oil, and garlic.

NESTING HABITS
Small plates will contain rows of around six, but large nestings may have up to twelve.

ORIGINS
Like most of China's pasta snacks, these probably were the invention of Hui Muslims who initially traveled across Northern China on the Silk Road. The most famous pot stickers are made in the northern port of Tianjin.

SPECIES
- **Beef Pot Stickers**
  牛肉鍋貼
  níuròu guōtiē · *ngau⁴ juk⁶ wo¹ tip³*
  Seasoned ground beef instead of pork.

- **Pan-Fried Steamed Jiaozi**
  煎餃
  jiānjiǎo · *zin¹ gaau²*
  Often sold as pot stickers, these are browned steamed *jiaozi*.

SIU MAI

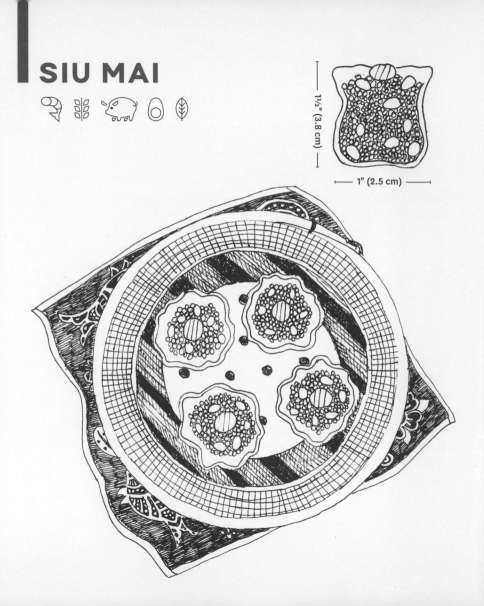

1½" (3.8 cm)

1" (2.5 cm)

GENUS 燒賣 · *shāomài* · *siu¹ maai⁶*

IDENTIFICATION Egg dough is formed into cups and filled with meat or rice. Invariably steamed, the sides of the *siu mai* are sometimes squeezed in to form a flower shape, and they sport a garnish of contrasting color sprinkled in the center. *Siu mai* almost always have a traditional Cantonese pork filling, although fancier teahouses sometimes offer a variety from different parts of China. Exterior is dry and tacky; interior is either meaty or starchy with chewy bits.

BASIC FILLING
Seasoned minced pork and sometimes shrimp, plus a scant amount of bamboo shoots, black mushrooms, and water chestnuts.

DEFAULT SAUCE OR DIP
Mix together soy sauce and mustard.

NESTING HABITS
Siu mai are often found in clusters of three to six in small bamboo steamer baskets, although groupings of four are the most common.

ORIGINS
Siu mai were enjoyed as long ago as the Yuan dynasty (1271 to 1368) in North China. Even to this day, *the* standard offerings in Cantonese-style teahouses are *siu mai*, Char Siu Buns (page 20), Custard Tarts (page 160), and Har Gow (page 34).

SPECIES
- **Shrimp Siu Mai**
  鮮蝦燒賣
  xiānxiā shāomài · *sin¹ haa¹ siu¹ maai⁶*
  Fresh shrimp, pork fat, and crunchy vegetables, frequently with a shrimp garnish.

- **Crab Siu Mai**
  蟹肉燒賣
  xièròu shāomài · *haai⁵ juk⁶ siu¹ maai⁶*
  Crabmeat and roe season the pork or shrimp filling; a pinch of orange roe accents the top.

- **Beef Siu Mai**
  牛肉燒賣
  niúròu shāomài · *ngau⁴ juk⁶ siu¹ maai⁶*
  These Northern-style pasta cups are stuffed with ground beef, ginger, and water chestnuts, and are topped with a single green pea.

- **Sticky Rice Siu Mai**
  糯米燒賣
  nuòmǐ shāomài · *no⁶ mai⁵ siu¹ maai⁶*
  Steamed, seasoned sticky rice mixed with bits of ham.

CHAR SIU
BUNS

2" (5 cm)

3" (7.5 cm)

GENUS 叉燒包 · *chāshāo bāo* · *caa¹ siu¹ baau¹*

IDENTIFICATION Springy, with a yeasty aroma, these *baozi* (filled and stuffed steamed buns) are wrapped with a special Cantonese dim sum bread dough so as to make the dough splay open into three or so shiny white "petals" that are craggy along the edges. The mahogany filling of chopped *char siu* (page 44) in a sweet sauce is visible between the petals.

Often sold in Chinese bakeries, as well as in just about any dim sum teahouse, the buns are protected by little paper squares on the bottom to keep them from sticking to the steamer. Exterior is fluffy with a smooth surface; interior is soft with chewy bits. Also called "barbecue pork buns," even though the pork never comes near an actual barbecue.

BASIC FILLING
Char siu seasoned with a light, sweet gravy of soy sauce, shallots, sugar, oyster sauce, hoisin sauce, and sesame oil.

DEFAULT SAUCE OR DIP
None.

NESTING HABITS
Often found in clusters of three or four in a medium-size bamboo steamer basket, although larger ones may nest alone in smaller baskets atop waxed paper squares; these bigger ones can often be sighted in Chinese bakeries.

ORIGINS
This bread dough is light, fluffy, and tensile, due to its assorted leavening agents. Cantonese *baozi* were first sold as snacks in Guangzhou teahouses. The classic description is "high in body with the shape of a sparrow's cage, a big belly that is firmly gathered up [at the top], and a mouth that explodes to ever-so-slightly reveal the filling."

SPECIES
• **Baked Char Siu Buns** (page 72)

CHICKEN
BUNS

2" (5 cm)

3" (7.5 cm)

GENUS 雞包仔 · *jī bāozǐ* · *gai¹ baau¹ zai²*

IDENTIFICATION Leavened dough is stuffed with boneless diced chicken. The surface is a shiny white, the bread is spongy and full of bubbles, and it can be made either with Char Siu Bun–style dough (page 20) that explodes into three or four "petals," or regular steamed bread dough (page 24) that remains sealed with a pleated rosette.

Chunks of juicy chicken—generally the thigh meat—are tossed with the contrasting flavors of sweet sausage or pork, as well as a good handful of aromatics. Exterior is fluffy with a smooth surface; interior is slightly tensile in a juicy gravy.

BASIC FILLING
The tender chicken is often combined with chewy bits of *lop chong* (sweet sausage) or pork, as well as green onions, cilantro, ginger, and a binding ingredient.

DEFAULT SAUCE OR DIP
None.

NESTING HABITS
These usually are seen in clusters of three or four nestled in medium-size bamboo steamer baskets, although larger ones may nest alone. The *baozi* settle on waxed paper squares; larger ones can be seen in Chinese bakeries.

ORIGINS
Chicken buns originated in Northern China. A legend says that the great strategist Zhuge Liang of the Three Kingdoms period invented steamed filled buns eighteen hundred years ago.

SPECIES
- **Big Chicken Buns**
  雞球大包
  jīqíu dàbāo · *gai¹ kau⁴ daai⁶ baau¹*
  An early variation on this genus found mainly along the busy streets of old Guangzhou. A main meal for the working poor, such as rickshaw pullers and laborers; the bones were left in so that diners could be assured that this was in fact not a furry substitute.

VEGETARIAN BUNS

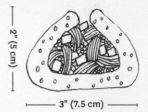

2" (5 cm)

3" (7.5 cm)

GENUS 素菜包 · *sùcài bāo* · *sou³ coi³ baau¹*

IDENTIFICATION Plain raised wheat dough is wrapped around a meatless filling with the edges pulled up to form a rosette on top. The best vegetarian buns will have crunchy things like toasted sesame seeds, aromatics such as green onion and ginger, and chewy bits of pressed bean curd. Exterior is fluffy with a smooth surface; interior is soft and juicy with crunchy morsels.

BASIC FILLING
Finely chopped, blanched green vegetables like bok choy are seasoned and mixed with ingredients that offer variety, such as minced pressed bean curd, cellophane noodles, and toasted sesame seeds.

DEFAULT SAUCE OR DIP
Mix together chile oil or sauce with soy sauce and vinegar.

NESTING HABITS
Three clustered together in a bamboo steamer basket, with either small waxed paper squares or steamer paper underneath; larger ones can be seen in Chinese bakeries.

ORIGINS
These most likely hail from Buddhist monasteries and temples in the Yangtze River environs, but like so many vegan dishes—such as Soy Skin Rolls (page 90)—these have been co-opted by carnivores with a passion simply because they are so delicious.

SPECIES
- **Curry Vegetarian Buns**
  咖喱素菜包
  kālí sùcài bāo · *gaa³ lei² sou³ coi³ baau¹*
  Chopped gluten or bean curd in a light curry sauce; finely diced carrots and black mushrooms are often added for color and texture.

- **Black Mushroom Buns**
  香菇素菜包
  xiānggū sùcài bāo · *hoeng¹ gu¹ sou³ coi³ baau¹*
  Chopped Chinese black mushrooms and occasionally some other varieties are mixed with soy sauce, sugar, rice wine, and green onions in a gravy; see Figurative Buns (page 142) for a beautiful variation.

CHAOZHOU
RICE ROLLS

1½" (3.8 cm)

2" (5 cm)

GENUS 潮州糯米卷 · *Cháozhōu nuòmǐ juǎn* · *Ciu⁴ zau¹ no⁶ mai⁵ gyun²*

IDENTIFICATION A seasoned sticky rice filling is wrapped with a leavened wheat dough, formed into long ropes, and then steamed. This dim sum is unusual in that the wrapper usually relies on baking powder rather than yeast, it is steamed in a long snake that is later cut, and the filling is not made from meat or vegetables.

Although on the surface this may appear to be just a starch stuffed with yet another starch, the reality is that the wrapper is slightly sweet and chewy, and this contrasts admirably with the soft, pillowy filling. Nuggets of pork and savory little chunks of mushrooms, peanuts, and so forth are seasoned with soy sauce, and the usual addition of pork fat to the sticky rice gives it a creamy mouthfeel. Exterior is dry and bouncy; interior is creamy and studded with a variety of savory ingredients.

BASIC FILLING
Steamed sticky rice mixed with soy sauce and finely diced seasonings that may include pork belly, Chinese black mushrooms, peanuts, salted radish, dried shrimp, and *lop chong* or other Chinese sausages.

DEFAULT SAUCE OR DIP
None.

NESTING HABITS
Three or four clustered together in a small bamboo steamer basket on top of steamer paper.

ORIGINS
Classic Chaozhou breakfast fare, these are enjoyed throughout northeastern Guangzhou, from markets to street stalls. These are usually accompanied by strong cups of the region's beloved oolong tea to complete the meal.

SPECIES
- **Fried Rice Rolls with Soy Skins**
  腐膜
  fǔmó · *fu⁶ mok⁶*
  Literally called "bean curd film" in the Chaozhou dialect, these possess the same filling as the main genus, but are wrapped with thin soy skins and lightly fried to crisp up the exterior. See Soy Skin Rolls (page 90) for another delicious way with this wrapper.

XIAOLONGBAO

1" (2.5 cm)

1" (2.5 cm)

GENUS 小籠包 · *xiǎolóng bāo* · *siu² lung⁵ baau¹*

IDENTIFICATION Named after the "little baskets" in which they appear, these Yangtze-style morsels always contain a good amount of jelled stock that melts as the meat filling steams. The most elegant examples of this genus are enclosed in paper-thin pasta dough made with hot water, which gives the surface an extraordinary tensile nature.

Pick these up by their topknot with your chopsticks and immediately cradle them in a spoon, as they should ideally be filled with searing hot juice. Exterior is smooth and tacky; interior is tensile and soupy. Sometimes referred to as "XLB" in English.

BASIC FILLING
Minced pork, jelled stock, and seasoning.

DEFAULT SAUCE OR DIP
Dark rice vinegar and thin shards of young ginger.

NESTING HABITS
Four or so are clustered inside a bamboo steamer basket, and nowadays are often nestled in small foil cups to help prevent them from tearing.

ORIGINS
One of the few non-Cantonese tea snacks to slide fairly recently into the dim sum hierarchy, *xiaolongbao* are natives of Jiangsu.

SPECIES

- **Crab Xiaolongbao**
  蟹粉小籠包
  xièfěn xiǎolóng bāo ·
  haai⁵ fan² siu² lung⁵ baau¹
  Crabmeat is mixed with ground pork and seasonings.

- **Crab Roe Xiaolongbao**
  蟹黃小籠包
  xièhuáng xiǎolóng bāo ·
  haai⁵ wong⁴ siu² lung⁵ baau¹
  Red crab roe provides a creamy edge to the seasoned pork filling.

- **Giant Soup Bun**
  灌湯包
  guàntāng bāo · *gun³ tong¹ baau¹*
  Found only at Shanghainese joints, these are simply massive steamed buns filled with broth. Pierce the top with a handy fat straw and sip away before munching on the rest.

CHEONG FUN

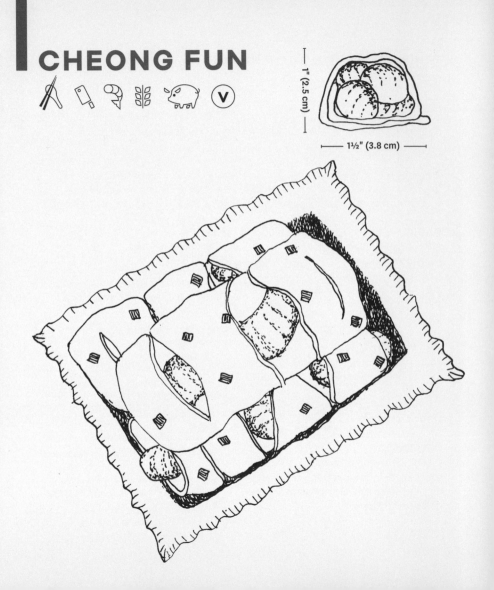

1" (2.5 cm)

1½" (3.8 cm)

GENUS 腸粉 · *chángfěn* · *coeng⁴ fan²*

IDENTIFICATION A large, thin steamed rice noodle is rolled around a filling of some sort. Wheat starch or cornstarch may be added to the freshly ground rice slurry to give it more of a tensile nature. Freshly made noodles lend the dish its lovely silkiness, and cilantro or sesame seeds often decorate the top. The name literally means "intestine [rice] noodles," for these glistening, lumpy sheets look somewhat like their namesake. Exterior is smooth and tacky; interior can be meaty or crunchy.

BASIC FILLING
Shrimp, *char siu*, roast duck, or a fried Chinese cruller.

DEFAULT SAUCE OR DIP
Sweetened soy sauce or savory meat juices.

NESTING HABITS
Usually found in clusters of three or four lazing against each other on an oval plate. Will be cut up into 1-inch (2.5-cm) pieces by the kitchen or server.

ORIGINS
The thin rice noodles probably came from the Pearl River Delta north of Hong Kong. By the late Qing dynasty (1644 to 1911), this dish was already being enjoyed in Guangzhou's teahouses and along her alleys.

SPECIES
- **Zhaliang**
  炸兩 · *zháliǎng* · *zaa³ loeng⁵*
  The soft rice noodle encloses a crispy fried cruller.

- **Shrimp-Stuffed Zhaliang**
  鮮蝦炸兩
  xiānxiā zháliǎng · *sin¹ haa¹ zaa³ loeng⁵*
  Minced fresh shrimp is stuffed inside the crullers.

- **Shrimp Cheong Fun**
  鮮蝦腸粉
  xiānxiā chángfěn · *sin¹ haa¹ coeng⁴ fan²*
  A seasoned shrimp stuffing with whole large fresh shrimp placed on top.

- **Roast Duck Cheong Fun**
  燒鴨腸粉
  shāoyā chángfěn · *siu¹ ngaap³ coeng⁴ fan²*
  This has the shredded meat and skin of Roast Duck (page 60) stuffed inside.

- **Char Siu Cheong Fun**
  叉燒腸粉
  chāshāo chángfěn · *caa¹ siu¹ coeng⁴ fan²*
  The filling is finely chopped Char Siu (page 44).

FUN GOR

¾" (1.9 cm)

1½" (3.8 cm)

GENUS 潮州粉粿 · *Cháozhōu fěnguǒ* · *Ciu⁴ zau¹ fan² gwo²*

IDENTIFICATION The jumbled fillings in these flattish steamed half-moons shimmer through the shiny, almost translucent surface. These unique wrappers are a mix of wheat starch and cornstarch, and so almost melt in the mouth. *Fun gor* have light, crumbly, nongreasy fillings made of dry, contrasting ingredients, and so raw *fun gor* rattle when shaken if they are made the classic way.

The Chinese name for these is usually "Chaozhou *fun gor*," to differentiate them from other treats that bear the same name. Try to get these freshly made, which ensures that the wrappers will be properly tensile, not sticky. Exterior is dry and slightly gluey; interior is a hodgepodge of delicious things that are crunchy and chewy.

BASIC FILLING
Finely diced pork, jicama, Chinese celery, black mushrooms, dried shrimp, peanuts, and cilantro.

DEFAULT SAUCE OR DIP
None.

NESTING HABITS
Usually found in clusters of three or four closely nestled together—but not touching—in a small steamer.

ORIGINS
The *fun gor* offered in teahouses belong to two main, though similar, species: that of Chaozhou, a fishing village in northern Guangdong on the border with Fujian, and that of the Pearl River Delta city of Shunde, just south of Guangzhou; the fillings of these two areas are what set the two varieties apart.

SPECIES
- **Shunde-Style Fun Gor**
  顺德粉粿
  Shùndé fěnguǒ · *Seon⁶ dak¹ fan² gwo²*
  Properly called 娥姐粉粿 · *Éjiě fěnguǒ* · *Ngo⁴ ze² fan² gwo²* after the woman (Ejie) who made these dim sum so famous, these creations have "thin wrappers like translucent glass so that the colors of the filling are discernable." These are generally stuffed with a mixture of finely diced pork, *char siu*, black mushrooms, fresh shrimp, and water chestnuts or jicama seasoned with oyster sauce and cilantro.

HAR GOW

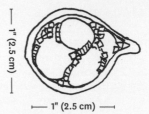

1" (2.5 cm)

1" (2.5 cm)

GENUS 蝦餃 · *xiā jiǎo* · *haa¹ gaau²*

IDENTIFICATION Multiple delicate folds on one side only give this delicacy its unique shape. It traditionally has twelve folds and a fat purse shape that Chinese gourmands have described as a "spider's belly." The bright pink color showing through the vaguely sticky and shiny exterior demonstrates why these divine dumplings truly deserve their Chinese name, "shrimp *jiaozi*."

A celebration of the exquisite quality of perfectly fresh shrimp, *har gow* are extraordinary when done right because there is simply no place for mediocre ingredients to hide. Exterior is dry and slightly tacky to the touch; interior is very crunchy and luscious.

BASIC FILLING
Pure chunks of fresh shrimp jumbled with tiny bits of pork fat and bamboo shoots.

DEFAULT SAUCE OR DIP
If you like, dab these very lightly in a mixture of mustard and soy sauce.

NESTING HABITS
Usually found in clusters of four closely nestled together, but never touching, in a small steamer.

ORIGINS
The wrappers are most likely a spin on the wheat-starch wrappers of Fun Gor (page 32). However, the filling was the inspired creation almost one hundred years ago of the Yizhen Teahouse.

Located on a tributary to the Pearl River, the chef at this famed eatery used the traditional culinary concept of seasonal dining (不時不食 · *bùshí bùshí* · *bat¹ si⁴ bat¹ sik⁶*) to develop these extraordinary morsels out of the day's freshest catch.

SPECIES
- **Single Shrimp Har Gow**
  獨蝦蝦餃
  dúxiā xiā jiǎo · *duk⁶ haa¹ haa¹ gaau²*
  Fat shrimp are marinated and then wrapped whole—one shrimp per dim sum—along with the minced fat and bamboo shoots, which makes the texture super snappy.

PORK AND MUNG BEAN TAMALES

3" (7.5 cm)

6" (15 cm)

GENUS 裹蒸粽 · lǐzhēngzòng · leoi⁵ zing¹ zung²

IDENTIFICATION Dried bamboo leaves form the interior wrapper for this tamale that is then rolled in lotus leaves and tied with kitchen string. Inside is a layer of sticky rice intertwined with the soft yellow strata of peeled mung beans that almost turn into a pudding as they absorb the fat from pork belly.

This is sometimes called 果裹蒸 · guǒlǐzhēng · gwo² leoi⁵ zing¹ if it has lots of extras inside, like chestnuts, brined egg yolks, lotus seeds, *lop chong*, peanuts, dried scallops, and black mushrooms. Exterior is covered with inedible leaves; interior is soft and sticky.

BASIC FILLING
Very soft sticky rice, strips of marinated pork belly, and hulled mung beans. Seasonings tend to include five-spice powder and fermented bean curd cheese.

DEFAULT SAUCE OR DIP
None.

NESTING HABITS
Usually found as a single nester on a round plate; the lotus leaves are removed to reveal the sticky tamale, which tends to be sliced open.

ORIGINS
Chinese tamales, or 粽子 · zòngzi · zung² zi², are as much a part of the Dragon Boat Festival (the fifth day of the fifth lunar month) as decorated cookies are a part of Christmas. It is said that when the patriot and poet Qu Yuan drowned himself over two millennia ago to protest political corruption, sympathetic commoners threw rice packets like these into the river to discourage the fish from nibbling on his body.

SPECIES
- **Zhaoqing Tamales**
  肇慶裹蒸粽
  Zhàoqìng lǐzhēngzòng · Siu⁶ hing³ leoi⁵ zing¹ zung²
  Named after a city in southern Guangdong, these are fundamentally the same as the main genus, but have a pyramid shape and weigh around a pound (450 g).

STICKY RICE CHICKEN IN LOTUS LEAVES

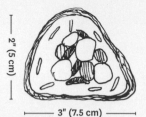

2" (5 cm)

3" (7.5 cm)

GENUS 糯米雞 • *nuòmǐ jī* • *no⁶ mai⁵ gai¹*

IDENTIFICATION Sticky rice is mixed with rich and funky seasonings, wrapped in dried lotus leaves into single-size servings, and steamed until tender. The leaf is not tied, but rather is folded up and nestled closely against others in a steamer.

The ideal version has a delicate balance of tender yet chewy thigh meat and deliciously seasoned rice. Exterior is an inedible leaf; interior is soft and sticky with textural contrasts from a wide variety of aromatics.

BASIC FILLING
Tender dark chicken meat is seasoned with chewy bits of black mushrooms and *lop chong* or pork, as well as soy sauce, oyster sauce, green onions, cilantro, and ginger, and sometimes featuring shreds of dried shrimp or scallops.

DEFAULT SAUCE OR DIP
None.

NESTING HABITS
Usually found in clusters of two to four, although sometimes this tamale-like offering morphs into a single, large packet.

ORIGINS
Most likely developed from the bamboo-wrapped rice tamales of the Hakka. First sold as small bowls, these snacks were later wrapped up to form simple take-away foods.

SPECIES
- **Lotus Leaf Rice**
荷葉飯
héyè fàn • *ho⁶ jip⁶ faan⁶*
A large packet of sticky rice is combined with chicken and other savory bits and wrapped in lotus leaves.

- **Pearl Chicken**
珍珠雞
zhēnzhū jī • *zan¹ zyu¹ gai¹*
Smaller than the main genus, this has bite-size pieces of poultry coated in soaked raw rice and seasonings, folded up in an untied lotus leaf, and steamed. This species probably evolved when some customers felt that they had been served too much starch and too little chicken.

- **Stuffed Chicken Wings**
糯米釀雞翅
nuòmǐ niàng jīchì • *no⁶ mai⁵ joeng⁶ gai¹ ci³*
Seasoned rice is packed into the boned middle joint of the wing, and both it and the wing tip are deep-fried until crunchy.

ROAST
SUCKLING PIG

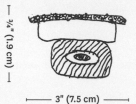

¾" (1.9 cm)

3" (7.5 cm)

GENUS 片皮烤乳豬 · *piànpí kǎo rǔzhū* · *pin³ pei⁴ haau¹ jyu⁵ zyu¹*

IDENTIFICATION Glossy, heavily shellacked mahogany skin gives this dish visual allure. Underneath that lies a layer of tender white fat and then a more diminutive layer of aromatic meat interspersed with small bones and cartilage. Before serving, the meat is cut into clean, even strips with sharp right angles by placing the meat skin-side down and then whacking through the piece with a razor-sharp cleaver.

The skin is crackly and crunchy thanks to the maltose (a syrup made from malt sugar) thinned with vinegar that lacquers the outside of this month-old piglet. Inside, the meat is seasoned with things like five-spice powder and Worcestershire sauce. Fancy banquets will supply tiny buns that allow you to turn this pork into an extraordinarily succulent sandwich, but teahouses almost inevitably go the simple route and serve the meat au naturel. Exterior is hard and crackly; interior is buttery and meaty with small bones.

DEFAULT SAUCE OR DIP
Sweetened soy sauce or savory meat juices.

NESTING HABITS
Prefers settling alone on a plate or platter, although it is sometimes spotted nesting on braised soybeans; on occasion small steamed buns will nestle alongside it. Can be found in Chinese delis.

ORIGINS
A delicacy now confined for the most part to Guangdong province and Hong Kong, suckling pig has been a beloved part of China's cuisines for at least two millennia. Some believe that its origins, therefore, lie in the north, probably between the Yellow and Yangtze Rivers.

SPECIES
- **Pockmarked Roast Suckling Pig**
  麻皮乳豬
  mápí rǔzhū · *maa⁴ pei⁴ jyu⁵ zyu¹*
  Cooked at a much higher temperature, this has oil rather than maltose brushed on the surface, which fries zillions of tiny bubbles into the surface of the golden skin.

CRACKLY SKINNED PORK BELLY

3" (7.5 cm)

⊢ 1" (2.5 cm) ⊣

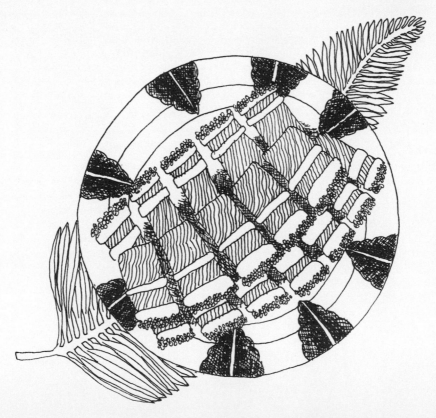

GENUS 燒肉 · *shāoròu* · *siu¹ juk⁶*

IDENTIFICATION Nubbly, hard, golden skin that tastes of divinely seasoned pork rinds contrasts with the thick slab of juicy pork lying underneath. The marvelous texture of the skin comes from frying or searing it a golden, bubbly brown; the meat is then hung in an oven where it is roasted until it is cooked to perfection. A large side of pork prepared this way usually hangs from a meat hook in the windows of places that specialize in 燒臘 · *shāolà* · *siu¹ laap⁶* ("roasted and cured meats").

Served warm, the meat is whacked into even squares or oblongs so that each piece has a good tile of the crunchy skin at one end, while the rest of each piece contains marbled layers of meat and fat. Exterior is crunchy and crisp; interior is buttery and deliciously meaty. Sometimes referred to either as 脆皮腩仔 · *cuìpí nǎnzǐ* · *ceoi³ pei⁴ naam⁵ zai²* ("crispy-skinned brisket") or 鑊底燒肉 · *huòdǐ shāoròu* · *wok⁶ dai² siu¹ juk⁶* ("wok-bottom roast meat").

DEFAULT SAUCE OR DIP
Occasionally has some roasting juices pooled on the plate or a thick bean sauce as a dip.

NESTING HABITS
Usually perches by itself on a porcelain plate and sometimes nests on braised soybeans. It can also be found roosting with some other roasted meats on an appetizer platter; dwells in Chinese delis, too.

ORIGINS
A native of the Guangzhou area, the range of this species is more or less limited to Cantonese-speaking environs. Specialty stores in Guangdong province offer it as part of an array of *shaola*, a family that includes charcuterie, as well as a wide variety of roasted ducks, chickens, and pork. Both Roast Suckling Pig (page 40) and crackly skinned pork belly belong to the same tiny branch of Cantonese *shaola* called 燒豬 · *shāozhū* · *siu¹ zyu¹*, which means "roast pork."

SPECIES
Sui generis.

CHAR SIU

1" (2.5 cm)

2" (5 cm)

GENUS 叉燒 · *chāshāo* · *caa¹ siu¹*

IDENTIFICATION The bright scarlet exterior of this sweetish meat sets it apart from all other varieties of Cantonese-style roast pork. Pork butt is the preferred cut for this dish, as it has the prized combination called "half fat and half lean" in Chinese. The marinated, boneless pork is carved into the characteristic ropes of *char siu*, as large ratios of surface to interior guarantees plenty of delectable blackened bits.

A good dollop of maltose—the thick liquid sugar that is the secret to the divine texture of many Chinese dishes—becomes a syrupy marinade for this pork when it is seasoned with soy sauce, five-spice powder, rice wine, garlic, and red fermented bean curd cheese. As just about any Cantonese child will tell you, the best parts of a slice of *char siu* are those blackened edges of meat candy. Exterior is scarlet, sweet, and savory, with a sticky sauce and caramelized parts; interior is pale gray and juicy.

DEFAULT SAUCE OR DIP
Sweetened soy sauce or savory meat juices.

NESTING HABITS
Usually nests alone on a small plate on top of braised soybeans, or it is fanned out on an appetizer plate with other meats; can be found in Chinese delis.

ORIGINS
Char siu is a Guangdong native and gets its name from the skewers (*char*) that the meat is threaded on before they are hung in an oven and roasted (*siu*).

SPECIES

- **Honey-Roasted Char Siu**
  蜜汁叉燒
  mìzhī chāshāo · *mat⁶ zap¹ caa¹ siu¹*
  This should contain honey rather than maltose.

- **Char Siu Pork Neck**
  叉燒豬頸肉
  chāshāo zhūjǐngròu · *caa¹ siu¹ zyu¹ geng²ᵘ juk⁶*
  Large pieces of boneless neck meat are roasted and then thinly sliced.

- **Char Siu Ribs**
  叉燒排骨
  chāshāo páigú · *caa¹ siu¹ paal⁴ gwat¹*
  Whole slabs of pork ribs are roasted and then whacked apart just before serving.

BLACK BEAN SPARERIBS

GENUS 豉汁排骨 · *chǐzhī páigú* · *si⁶ zap¹ paai⁴ gwat¹*

IDENTIFICATION Crosscut pork spareribs are sliced midway between each bone so that every portion is more or less a 1-inch (2.5-cm) cube. These are usually tossed with starch, quickly stir-fried, and then steamed with fermented black beans, ginger, and other aromatics until tender. May have chiles present.

The meat is extremely juicy and flavorful, with chewy tendons around the bone. The exterior should be silky from the starch coating and studded with lots of black beans and garlic; the interior is juicy and very meaty, and contains small lengths of bone and tendons.

DEFAULT SAUCE OR DIP
Juices from the steamed meat plus a pleasing array of aromatics.

NESTING HABITS
These ribs nest in a pile inside a rimmed saucer that is then encased in a small steamer basket.

ORIGINS
Most non-Muslim areas of China have their own take on steamed or braised spareribs. Since many of Guangdong's most classic dishes—such as Fried Rice (page 106) and Fried Wontons (page 93)—were derived from cuisines along the lower Yangtze River, this Cantonese iteration might have received its inspiration from there and then evolved over the years in Guangdong, using local seasonings like fermented black beans, which are not commonly used along the Yangtze, but rather in Hunan and points south.

SPECIES
• **Steamed Spareribs with Preserved Olives**
欖角蒸排骨
lǎnjiǎo zhēng páigú ·
laam⁵ gok³ zing¹ paai⁴ gwat¹
Chopped cured Chinese olives season the pork instead of the black beans.

• **Steamed Spareribs with Plum Sauce**
梅子蒸排骨
méizi zhēng páigú ·
mui⁴ zi² zing¹ paai⁴ gwat¹
Salted plum sauce takes the place of the black beans in this Chaozhou-style specialty.

STEAMED
MEATBALLS

1" (2.5 cm)

1" (2.5 cm)

GENUS 蒸肉丸子 · *zhēng ròuwánzi* · *zing¹ juk⁶ jyun² zi²*

IDENTIFICATION Finely minced fatty pork is rolled into meatballs without any added crust or coating. The meatballs then are steamed until juicy and fragrant. The pork becomes very tender yet tensile, and the bowl becomes filled with savory juices.

Each teahouse will have its own take on this classic. Crunchy bits of coarsely chopped water chestnut or Chinese celery often speckle the meat, while others might feature bits of black mushroom or bamboo shoots. Exterior and interior of each ball are composed of juicy, springy meat interspersed with tiny nuggets of crispy, diced vegetables.

DEFAULT SAUCE OR DIP
A puddle of the meatballs' own juices.

NESTING HABITS
Generally nests in groups of three or four in a little bowl that is itself enclosed in a small bamboo steamer basket to keep them warm.

ORIGINS
Meatballs are found in every corner of China, with Muslim areas depending upon lamb and goat instead of pork, and vegetarian enclaves along the Yangtze using bean curd or gluten as the main ingredient. The meatballs are invariably seasoned in a way that reflects local tastes. Some become quite large—like the lion head meatballs of Jiangsu—and the meat is then lightened with a starch that turns this meatball into a delectable sponge.

SPECIES
- **Pearl Meatballs**
  珍珠丸子
  zhēnzhū wánzi · *zan¹ zyu¹ jyun² zi²*
  Natives of northern Hubei along the Yangtze River, these meatballs are raw pork mixed with chopped water chestnuts, rolled in raw sticky rice, and steamed; usually served with a dipping sauce.

- **Beef Meatballs**
  牛肉丸子
  niúròu wánzi · *ngau⁴ juk⁶ jyun² zi²*
  Most likely derived by Chaozhou cooks from a traditional Hakka dish, these poached meatballs are so bouncy that they often squeak against the teeth. Can be eaten with a dipping sauce.

STUFFED
BEAN CURD

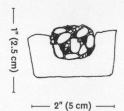

1" (2.5 cm)

2" (5 cm)

GENUS 釀豆腐 · *niàng dòufŭ* · *joeng⁶ dau⁶ fu⁶*

IDENTIFICATION A specialty of the Hakka areas in the inland mountainous regions of Guangdong, Fujian, and Jiangxi, bean curd (tofu) is hollowed out and stuffed before being braised or steamed. The filling is usually pork, although fish paste or shrimp may be included. The filling side is generally pan-fried—or the entire packet deep-fried—before the braising or steaming.

Variations on this include stuffed eggplant, lotus root, bitter melon, chile peppers, sweet peppers, and so forth. Exterior is soft and supple, or deep-fried and chewy; interior is juicy, savory, and in high contrast to the exterior.

DEFAULT SAUCE OR DIP
Savory gravy seasoned with soy sauce and ginger.

NESTING HABITS
Six or so pieces huddled together in a bowl and swimming in sauce.

ORIGINS
The Hakka people are widely credited with creating stuffed bean curd after they moved to South China from the Yellow River area. Since wheat wrappers were no longer available for their beloved Jiaozi (page 14), bean curd came to be used instead—culinary Darwinism in action. Now many cuisines south of the Yangtze include stuffed bean curd and vegetables as staples in their repertoire, including Sichuan, Guangxi, and Hubei. These are often deep-fried and then cooked in a sauce, or else braised, as is done here.

SPECIES
- **Stuffed Chile Peppers**
  釀辣椒
  niàng làjiāo · *joeng⁶ laat⁶ ziu¹*
  Jalapeño or milder chile peppers are cut in half, seeded, and filled with the forcemeat.

- **Stuffed Eggplant**
  釀茄子
  niàng qiézi · *joeng⁶ ke⁴ zi¹*
  Thick slices of unpeeled Chinese or Japanese eggplant sandwich the filling.

- **Stuffed Clams**
  蛤蜊燒賣
  géli shāomài · *gaap³ lei⁴ siu¹ maai⁶*
  The clams are steamed open, and their meat is mixed with pork, shrimp, black mushrooms, and aromatics before being stuffed back into the shells and then steamed once again.

BRAISED BRISKET WITH RADISHES

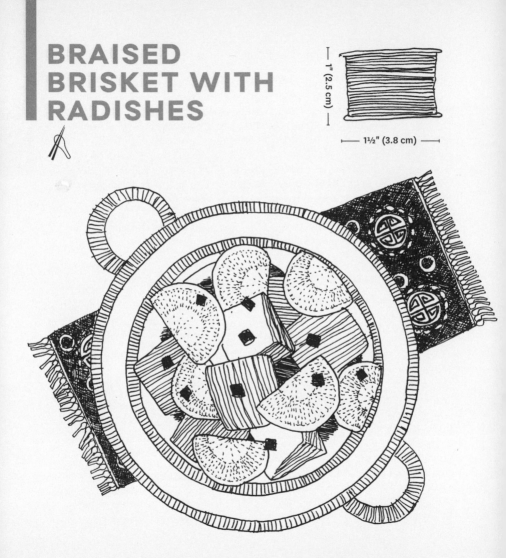

GENUS 蘿蔔牛腩煲 · *luóbó niúnǎn bào* · *lo⁴ baak⁶ ngau⁴ naam⁵ bou¹*

IDENTIFICATION Chunks of beef brisket are braised until tender in a rich sauce seasoned with soy sauce, rice wine, and ginger. The connective tissues in this tough yet very flavorful cut of meat remain a bit rubbery in some places, while others partially dissolve into the sauce, and this in turn makes the broth slightly sticky on the lips. Cubes of Chinese radish add a sweet counterbalance. A soupy sauce grounds the dish and flavors it with a good range of aromatics that vary according to the kitchen's predilections. Portions are steamed in bowls prior to serving and usually given a green onion or cilantro garnish.

The meat is relatively lean and tender, and it is often edged with chewy ribbons of the more tensile pale collagen that weaves through this cut of beef; the radishes are plump, flavorful, and sweet. Chinese radishes are sometimes erroneously referred to as "turnips" in English.

DEFAULT SAUCE OR DIP
Savory meat juices.

NESTING HABITS
A jumble of meat, vegetables, and sauce piled into either a casserole or a small bowl centered in a bamboo steamer basket.

ORIGINS
Probably introduced to South China from the cold North, this dish is very similar to Beijing's red-cooked beef dishes that likewise contrast stewed beef with fresh radishes. Curry was most likely added to certain Cantonese dishes when the British brought their taste for this spice mix from India to the treaty port of Guangzhou.

SPECIES
- **Braised Tripe**
  潷牛肚
  lǔ niúdǔ · *lou⁵ ngau⁴ tou⁵*
  Honeycomb tripe is the preferred variety. Soy sauce, rice wine, sugar, aromatics, and Chinese herbs lend the tender ribbons a golden hue.

- **Curry Beef Tripe**
  咖喱金錢肚
  kālí jīnqián dǔ · *gaa³ lei² gam¹ cin⁴ tou⁵*
  Honeycomb tripe is braised in a light curry sauce, generally with chunks of potatoes.

ROAST
CHICKEN

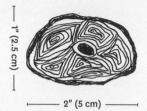

1" (2.5 cm)

2" (5 cm)

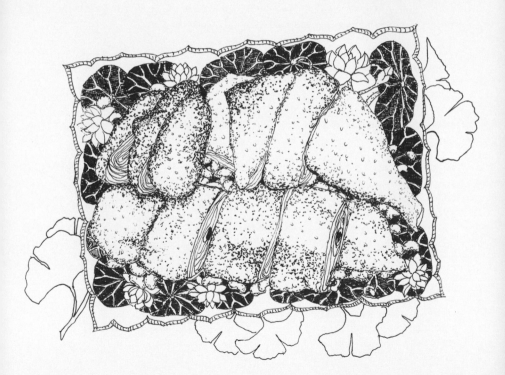

GENUS 燒雞 · _shāo jī_ · _siu¹ gai¹_

IDENTIFICATION Whole birds are marinated with either salt or soy sauce, and seasonings can include five-spice and sand ginger, as well as aromatics such as green onions and fresh ginger. The chickens are then hung up by hooks through their heads and roasted in an oven until the skin is crispy or sticky and the meat is tender and juicy. The feet are usually removed and cooked separately in a braise of some sort.

Marinade is air-dried on the birds before they are roasted, which lacquers the surface as the fat melts. The oven's hot air then balloons up under the skin and turns it into a crispy, sweet layer over the juicy flesh. Roast chicken sometimes has fried shrimp chips on the side. Exterior is brittle or sticky and often lightly sweet; interior is moist and savory.

DEFAULT SAUCE OR DIP
Sweetened soy sauce or spiced meat juices.

NESTING HABITS
A quarter, half, or whole bird is chopped into chunks and served on a plate; deeper-hued varieties will often be nestled on top of braised soybeans or shrimp chips. Can be found in Chinese delis.

ORIGINS
Other than salt-baked chicken, the ancestors of this genus were most likely introduced from Eastern China to Guangzhou, where they evolved into new species.

SPECIES
- **Pipa Chicken**
  琵琶雞
  pípá jī · pei⁴ paa⁴ gai¹
  The bird is butterflied down the front so that the head remains attached to the spine, and then it is skewered open before being hung over a fire.

- **Salt-Baked Chicken**
  鹽焗雞
  yánjú jī · jim¹ guk⁶ gai¹
  A Hakka specialty, the bird is wrapped in paper and buried in hot salt, which slowly roasts the chicken; always served with a hot oil dip seasoned with salt, shredded ginger, and minced green onions.

BRAISED
CHICKEN

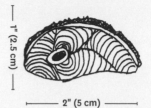

1" (2.5 cm)

2" (5 cm)

GENUS 滷雞 · *lǔ jī* · *lou⁵ gai¹*

IDENTIFICATION A whole chicken is slowly cooked in broth seasoned with ginger, green onion, sand ginger, black pepper, and traditional Chinese herbs. The sauce may be slightly sweet or deeply savory. The bird is generally poached over very low heat to keep the meat tender and to prevent the skin from tearing. Unlike Roast Chicken (page 54), the fat and skin remain attached to the meat. It is often hung up to dry a bit and then chopped before serving. Exterior is slightly sticky and glossy; interior is juicy and contains bones.

DEFAULT SAUCE OR DIP
Savory meat juices for the dark varieties; lighter birds are often accompanied by bowls of shredded ginger and green onions bathed in hot oil and salt.

NESTING HABITS
A quarter, half, or whole bird is chopped into chunks and served on a plate; deeper-hued varieties will often be perched on a scattering of braised soybeans.

ORIGINS
Most probably traveled to Guangdong from Eastern China, where red-cooked and poached chickens are still enjoyed to this day.

SPECIES

- **Poached Chicken**
  白切雞
  báiqiē jī · *baak⁶ cit³ gai¹*
  A bird cooked in a pale broth, this subgenus includes Consort's Chicken 貴妃雞 · *guìfēi jī* · *gwai³ fei¹ gai¹*.

- **Master Sauce Chicken**
  豉油雞
  chǐyóu jī · *si⁶ jau⁴ gai¹*
  The bright, dark skin and juicy flesh are courtesy of a rich, seasoned soy sauce broth.

- **Crispy-Skinned Chicken**
  脆皮雞
  cuìpí jī · *ceoi³ pei⁴ gai¹*
  Pale poached chicken is coated with a maltose mixture and then fried until reddish and crunchy; usually served with fried shrimp chips.

- **Magistrate's Chicken**
  太爺雞
  tàiyé jī · *taai³ je⁴ gai¹*
  Smoked master sauce chicken.

PROTEINS

BLACK BEAN
CHICKEN FEET

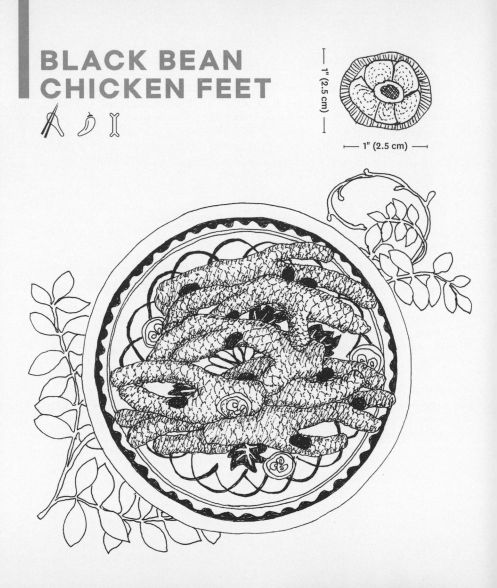

GENUS 豉汁鳳爪 · *chǐzhī fèngzhuǎ* · *si⁶ zap¹ fung⁶ zaau²*

IDENTIFICATION Whole chicken feet with the nails removed and a small bit above the ankle attached make this, at least to the uninitiated, one of the strangest-looking of all dim sum dishes. Admittedly, there is zero meat to be had here. However, these feet are a mainstay in teahouses for the simple reason that they taste absolutely delicious thanks to the flavorful sauce that seeps into every cranny, and the meatless bits offer wonderful texture for the teeth, tongue, and lips to play with. Beneath the fluffy skin is a layer of slightly sticky tendons.

Most often, the seasonings are rich with garlic, fermented black beans, and chiles. Many small bones need to be removed as the feet are eaten—from longer toe bones to tiny bits the size of watermelon seeds—so this dish is usually consumed in small bites with the chopsticks and spoon close to the mouth to convey the food and bones back and forth. Exterior is soft and supple; interior consists of slightly chewy tendons surrounding the bones. Referred to by the euphemism "phoenix claws" in both dialects.

DEFAULT SAUCE OR DIP
Savory meat juices.

NESTING HABITS
A pile of five to seven feet are arranged neatly on a rimmed plate; sometimes found in Chinese delis.

ORIGINS
All parts of an animal are treated with respect in Chinese kitchens, and this has been true since the country's earliest records of who ate what and where. Nothing is, therefore, ever wasted, but rather cooked in ways that highlight its innate textures and flavors. Chicken feet are no exception. Enjoyment of their distinctive pleasures probably traveled from North China, but this particular way with avian toes is unmistakably a Cantonese delight.

SPECIES
- **White-Braised Chicken Feet**
  白滷鳳爪
  báilǔ fèngzhuǎ · *baak⁶ lou⁵ fung⁶ zaau²*
  The prepared feet are poached in a clear broth seasoned with herbs, such as black cardamom and bay leaves.

ROAST
DUCK

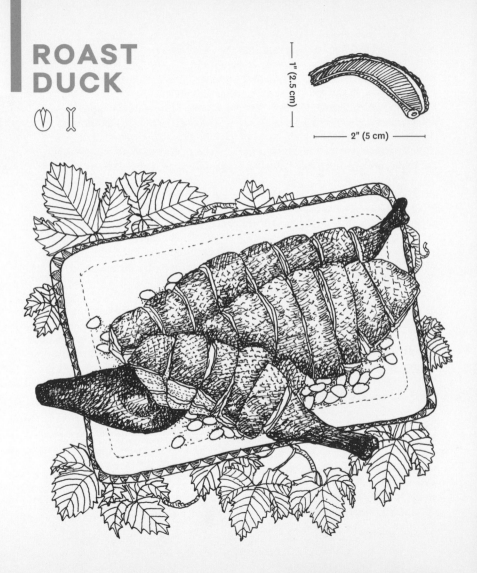

1" (2.5 cm)

2" (5 cm)

GENUS 燒鴨 · *shāo yā* · *siu¹ ngaap³*

IDENTIFICATION Cantonese roast duck has a shiny, mahogany-hued skin; an abundance of seasonings like fresh ginger, sand ginger, and five-spice in the cavity; and dark, juicy meat. The whole bird is eviscerated, and the lower two joints of the wings and the feet are removed to keep them from charring. It is blanched, and the duck is then shellacked with maltose and hung from a metal hook by the head in a special oven, where it is roasted, its melting fat acting as the basting juices.

These birds are usually displayed in the front window of a deli or in a kitchen window at a teahouse, and then chopped to order, although dim sum carts may also offer them already cut up. A scattering of braised soybeans or peanuts often is hidden underneath. Exterior is crisp and sweet; interior is moist, savory, and spiced.

DEFAULT SAUCE OR DIP
Sweetened soy sauce or savory meat juices.

NESTING HABITS
A quarter, half, or whole bird is chopped into chunks and served on a plate, often nestled on top of braised soybeans; always offered in Chinese delis.

ORIGINS
Guangzhou is famed for its roast duck, and Southern chefs very likely brought this dish with them from the capital, where it was known as Peking duck, a royal treat that has been around for at least fifteen hundred years.

SPECIES
- **Pipa Duck**
  琵琶鴨
  pípá yā · *pei⁴ paa⁴ ngaap³*
  The duck is opened up on the breast side and flattened before being roasted.

- **Chaozhou-Style Braised Duck**
  潮州鹵水鴨
  Cháozhōu lǔshuǐ yā ·
  Ciu⁴ zau¹ lou⁵ seoi² ngaap³
  This deeper-hued bird is slowly poached in soy sauce, rock sugar, and warm spices, such as star anise and cinnamon.

- **Roast Goose** · 燒鵝 · *shāo é* · *siu¹ ngo⁴*
  A specialty of Nanning, the capital of Guangxi to the west of Guangdong. Geese are more expensive than duck, and so are not as common; their preparation is very similar to that of roast duck.

BRAISED
DUCK CHINS

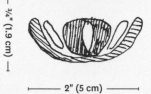

3/4" (1.9 cm)

2" (5 cm)

GENUS 滷鴨下巴 · *lǔ yāxiàbā* · *lou⁵ ngaap³ haa⁵ baa¹*

IDENTIFICATION The lower half of the duck head, including the bottom bill and tongue, are cut off beneath the brain and then slowly cooked in a savory broth of soy sauce, rice wine, rock sugar, warm spices like star anise and cinnamon, and aromatics such as fresh ginger and green onions. The tough meat slowly becomes tender and infused with all of these flavors, and the bills can be used as handles to pick up each piece for nibbling; foil is sometimes wrapped around the ends of the bill for tidy dining.

To eat these, hold the large, meaty end with your chopsticks and the tip of the bill with the fingertips of your other hand, and use your teeth to rip open the bill. Then, nibble on one half of the lower bill at a time. The tongue has a large, Y-shaped bone inside, but otherwise you're just going to eat around the beak. The bills are hard and inedible, but the tongues and other meaty bits are gently chewy and tasty.

DEFAULT SAUCE OR DIP
Sweetened soy sauce or savory meat juices.

NESTING HABITS
Four to six "chins" arrayed in a starburst pattern on a plate. The tongues are often braised by themselves and sold in Chinese delis.

ORIGINS
As with the rest of China, Guangdong and Hong Kong take pride in enjoying seemingly disposable parts of the animal to their fullest. This is absolute head-to-toe dining at its most creative and delicious.

SPECIES
- **Braised Duck Chins in Maggi Sauce**
  美極鴨下巴
  Měijí yāxiàbā · *Mei⁵ gik⁶ ngaap³ haa⁵ baa¹*
  Same as the main genus, but with additional deep flavors provided by the Swiss hydrolyzed protein sauce called Maggi Seasoning. These are also delicious when coated in batter, deep-fried, and then tossed with a slightly sweet-sour sauce seasoned with Maggi.

- **Braised Duck Feet**
  滷鴨掌
  lǔ yāzhǎng · *lou⁵ ngaap³ zoeng²*
  Very similar to Black Bean Chicken Feet (page 58), but this variety is simply braised in the same sauce as the main genus.

BLANCHED GOOSE INTESTINES

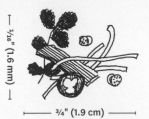

1/16" (1.6 mm)

3/4" (1.9 cm)

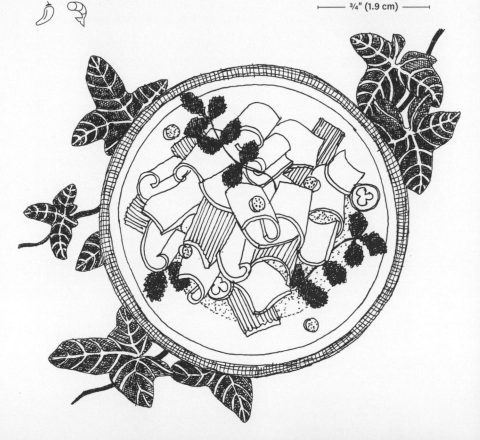

GENUS 白灼鵝腸 · *báizhuó écháng* · *baak⁶ coek³ ngo⁴ coeng⁴*

IDENTIFICATION Pure white strips of thin, almost papery, flesh are steamed with chiles or celery, and they might be sprinkled with a garnish of green onions or cilantro. When done correctly, the intestines are completely opened up to create flat ribbons. These are cleaned thoroughly and blanched, which preserves their gently crunchy character. The ribbons are then tossed with seasonings like oyster sauce, sesame oil, rice wine, and Sichuan peppercorns, all of which tame the gaminess of this cut of meat.

The intestines themselves end up relatively flavorless, but they serve as excellent sponges for the zesty seasonings. The strips are gently chewy and smooth; the contrasting vegetables will be either crisp or powerfully flavored.

DEFAULT SAUCE OR DIP
Savory juices will collect in the bottom of the bowl, and a small bowl of chile sauce or other dip may accompany it.

NESTING HABITS
Tangles of the flat meat are intertwined with vegetables in a small bowl.

ORIGINS
China is home to the whole hog—or in this case, whole bird—school of culinary philosophy. Intestines, especially from pigs and poultry, are beloved in almost every Chinese cuisine. This recipe may very well have been adapted from an Eastern Chinese recipe, as its seasoning is particularly delicate.

SPECIES
- **Braised Goose Intestines**
  滷水鵝腸
  lǔshuǐ écháng · *lou⁵ seoi⁸ ngo⁴ coeng⁴*
  The intestines are prepared in much the same way as Braised Duck Chins (page 62).

- **Stir-Fried Goose Intestines**
  炒鵝腸
  chǎo écháng · *caau² ngo¹ coeng⁴*
  Green onions and shredded fresh ginger are often the perfect accompaniment.

BRAISED
CUTTLEFISH

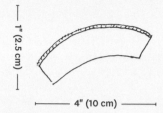

1" (2.5 cm)

4" (10 cm)

GENUS 滷墨魚 · *lŭ mòyú* · *lou⁵ mak⁶ jyu⁴*

IDENTIFICATION Shaped somewhat like a squid, this sea creature is rounder and much meatier. A whole cuttlefish is quickly poached in a very savory braising liquid, as long cooking will toughen the flesh, and then soaked in the cooled cooking sauce, which gives the outer edge a deep mahogany hue. These are often sold by the animal, unless they are very large, and so the cook will clean the cooked cuttlefish and then slice it diagonally into thin pieces just before serving. A cuttlefish body has a mild flavor and a very silky texture when prepared correctly, although the tentacles tend to be delightfully chewy. The exterior is a savory reddish brown; the interior is a clean-tasting pure white.

DEFAULT SAUCE OR DIP
Some of the braising liquid is usually all that is needed.

NESTING HABITS
Thin slices are fanned across a whole lettuce leaf, or else presented au naturel with a sprig of parsley. Often seen in Chinese delis as huge, whole cuttlefish colored neon orange.

ORIGINS
Guangdong and Southern Fujian seem to love this seafood more than any other place in China, and so there are many recipes for it, but braising is the preparation of choice in dim sum restaurants.

SPECIES

- **Chaozhou-Style Braised Cuttlefish**
  潮州滷墨魚
  Cháozhōu lŭ mòyú · *Ciu⁴ zau¹ lou⁵ mak⁶ jyu⁴*
  The cuttlefish are quickly poached in a very flavorful marinade that includes fish sauce, white liquor, and a large handful of aromatic spices.

- **Braised Baby Octopus**
  滷八爪魚
  lŭ bāzhuǎyú · *lou⁵ baat³ zaau² jyu⁴*
  Tiny whole octopuses are gently simmered in a flavorful sauce.

COLD TOSSED JELLYFISH

¼" (6.4 mm)

3" (7.5 cm)

GENUS 涼拌海蜇 · *liángbàn hǎizhé* · *loeng⁴ bun³ hoi² zat⁶*

IDENTIFICATION Thin ribbons of blanched jellyfish are tossed in an aromatic dressing. Both the "heads" (the oral arms) and the "skin" (the hood) are used, although they have completely different textures. The "skin" is most commonly seen in Chinese restaurants, as it is flat and smooth, and it combines well with slender shreds of cucumbers and other mild vegetables like carrots, as well as a sprinkling of toasted sesame seeds. The "heads" look more like cauliflower florets and are much crunchier in texture.

In this dish, sesame oil, rice vinegar, sugar, thinly sliced fresh chiles, and chopped garlic usually season the jellyfish, which have almost no taste of their own. Rather, they are beloved for their slightly crisp texture and silky mouthfeel—much like latex bands that somehow had life breathed into them—and so this dish offers many contrasts in consistency and flavor. The jellyfish are tensile, crisp, and bland; the vegetables are gently crunchy and either tannic or highly aromatic.

DEFAULT SAUCE OR DIP
Sweetened vinegar with a touch of salt.

NESTING HABITS
These always appear as shiny tangles on a plate, with whatever vegetables that are accompanying them closely intertwined with the jellyfish.

ORIGINS
The main type of jellyfish used for food in China is the scyphozoan, a plump, flattish jellyfish with short oral arms trailing under the wide, bell-shaped hood. Sometimes referred to as the "true" jellyfish, these are cleaned and salted for the Chinese market. To prepare them for eating, the jellyfish are soaked for a couple of days in many changes of freshwater before being sliced and quickly blanched; no other cooking is necessary or desirable.

SPECIES
- **Cold Jellyfish with Seaweed**
  海草海蜇
  hǎicǎo hǎizhé · *hoi² cou² hoi² zat⁶*
  Thin ribbons of blanched green seaweed tumble through the dish instead of—or sometimes in addition to—the cucumbers.

RADISH PUFFS

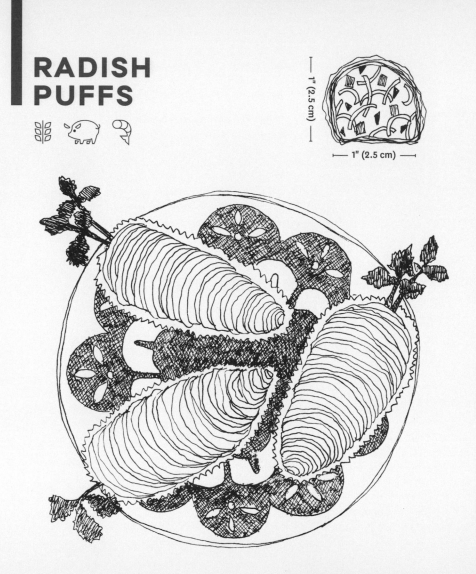

1" (2.5 cm)

1" (2.5 cm)

GENUS 蘿蔔酥 · *luóbó sū* · *lo⁴ baak⁶ sou¹*

IDENTIFICATION Chinese radish is grated into very thin strips and stir-fried with savory items. The vegetable retains its individual character, as it is barely cooked through, and so turns into silky threads that form a bland backdrop for a sprinkle of powerfully flavored seasonings.

Chinese puff pastry is then wrapped in a spiral around the seasoned shredded radish threads and baked until golden, which expands the wrapper into a crispy pleated exterior that shatters when bitten into. Sometimes greens (like sprigs of parsley) are stuck in one end to make it look even more like a root vegetable. Exterior is crunchy and dry; interior is soft and savory.

BASIC FILLING
Chinese radish, Chinese ham or dried shrimp, green onions, and black pepper.

DEFAULT SAUCE OR DIP
None.

NESTING HABITS
Clustered in groups of three on a plate inside individual paper cups.

ORIGINS
These very possibly developed from the baked radish pastries (蘿蔔酥餅 · *luóbó sūbǐng* · *lo⁴ baak⁶ sou¹ beng²*) of the lower Yangtze River area. Although those are also wrapped in Southern-style puff pastry, they are smooth and round, and topped with sesame seeds.

SPECIES

• **Deep-Fried Radish Puffs**
炸蘿蔔酥
zhá luóbó sū · *zaa³ lo⁴ baak⁶ sou¹*
Identical to baked radish puffs, except that they are deep-fried.

• **Carrot Puffs**
紅蘿蔔酥
hóngluóbó sū · *hung⁴ lo⁴ baak⁶ sou¹*
As the name suggests, these substitute carrots for radishes in this relatively new variation.

BAKED CHAR SIU BUNS

1" (2.5 cm)

2" (5 cm)

GENUS 焗叉燒包 · *jú chāshāo bāo* · *guk⁶ caa¹ siu¹ baau¹*

IDENTIFICATION Parker House dinner roll–type sweet raised dough is wrapped around a sweet, meaty filling. The top is often glazed with an egg wash. These have the folds on the bottom so that the top is smooth and shiny. A somewhat more modern member of the dim sum family, baked *char siu* buns have a distinctive Western edge to them, as buttery baked buns point to an almost American influence, but it is one that somehow melds beautifully with the very Chinese filling.

Exterior is fluffy, smooth, and yeasty; interior is sweet and soft with little chewy bits. These sometimes are sold as 叉燒餐包 · *chāshāo cānbāo* · *caa¹ siu¹ caan¹ baau¹* ("*char siu* dinner rolls").

BASIC FILLING
See Char Siu Buns (page 20).

DEFAULT SAUCE OR DIP
None.

NESTING HABITS
Three huddled on a plate, sometimes on top of a doily; larger ones can be seen in Chinese bakeries.

ORIGINS
These evolved in Guangdong and Hong Kong from traditional steamed *char siu* buns and probably were influenced by Western baked goods.

SPECIES

- **Crispy Char Siu Puffs**
  脆皮叉燒酥
  cuìpí chāshāo sū · *ceoi³ pei⁴ caa¹ siu¹ sou¹*
  Southern-style puff pastry is folded around the filling, brushed with an egg wash, and sprinkled with sesame seeds. Can be oblong or crescent shaped.

- **Crumbly Baked Char Siu Buns**
  酥皮焗叉燒包
  sūpí jú chāshāo bāo · *sou¹ pei⁴ guk⁶ caa¹ siu¹ baau¹*
  A shortbreadlike crust surrounds the *char siu* filling in these larger round buns.

- **Snow-Topped Char Siu Buns**
  雪山叉燒包
  xuéshān chāshāo bāo · *syut³ saan¹ caa¹ siu¹ baau¹*
  Very airy stuffed bread crowned with a brittle topping, as in the sweet genus known as Snow-Topped Buns (page 140).

BAKED

CURRY BEEF TURNOVERS

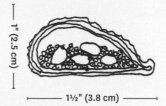

1" (2.5 cm)

1½" (3.8 cm)

GENUS 咖喱角 · *kālí jiǎo* · *gaa³ lei² gok³*

IDENTIFICATION Rounds of Southern-style puff pastry enclose ground beef and curry. The edges are crimped together to form a half-moon. The beauty of this dish lies in the shell-like pattern that appears once it is baked. Ground beef is rarely used in Southern Chinese cooking, and combining it with curry powder is as rare as Halley's Comet just about anywhere in the country, which signals that foreign inspirations are at work here.

Some versions prefer to use a short pastry dough that is dabbed with an egg wash and sprinkled with sesame seeds, while others fold the filling into spring roll skin triangles before frying. Exterior is crispy and flaky; interior is juicy, crumbly, and meaty. Also called "curry puffs" (咖喱卜 · *kālí bǔ* · *gaa³ lei² buk¹*) in Cantonese and English; the use of the foreign-sounding *buk* for "puffs" in its name highlights the strong Indian and British influences.

BASIC FILLING
Ground beef is fried with finely chopped onions and then mixed with a touch of sugar, salt, and a thin gravy seasoned with curry powder.

DEFAULT SAUCE OR DIP
None.

NESTING HABITS
Three or so corralled on a plate, each in its own paper cup or on a doily; larger ones can be seen in Chinese bakeries.

ORIGINS
The flavor, shape, and texture are very similar to those of India's samosas, and so these were perhaps developed in Guangzhou and Hong Kong as a result of Britain's lengthy hold on these two areas. Curry occasionally finds its way into a couple of other dishes, especially in former foreign enclaves like Macau, Hong Kong, and Fuzhou.

SPECIES
• **Curry Vegetarian Turnovers**
  素菜咖喱角
  sùcài kālí jiǎo · *sou³ coi³ gaa³ lei² gok³*
  Mashed potatoes take the place of beef in this Chinese riff on the samosa.

CREAMY CABBAGE CASSEROLE

3" (7.5 cm)

4" (10 cm)

GENUS 奶油焗白菜 · *nǎiyóu jú báicài* · *naai⁵ jau⁴ guk⁶ baak⁶ coi³*

IDENTIFICATION A bubbling casserole—either large or individual serving size—of tender hearts of napa cabbage in a cream sauce typifies the best renderings of this dish. This is similar to a béchamel sauce and calls upon either fresh cream or evaporated milk thickened with flour and butter to form a velvety, luscious background for the soft cabbage.

The cabbage is well drained before it is tossed the glossy sauce to preserve the béchamel's textural allure. Sometimes topped with grated Parmesan cheese, this casserole is best when the thick yet luscious sauce is browned on top into a leopard pattern. Exterior is chewy and sometimes cheesy; interior molten hot with silky ribbons of cabbage and tiny savory bits.

BASIC FILLING
Blanched hearts of napa cabbage, cream sauce, diced onions, and either dried scallops or minced Chinese ham.

DEFAULT SAUCE OR DIP
None.

NESTING HABITS
Always served in either a sandpot or heatproof dish, as it is heated up and browned just before serving. These can serve from one to four people, depending upon the size.

ORIGINS
Most likely another variation on a British dish, as cream sauces are not indigenous to China, but with the inevitable Chinese twist courtesy of the cabbage hearts and savory touches. Chefs will often show off a personal flair with this dish, perhaps dusting it with cheese, or jacking up the savory flavors with shreds of ham or dried scallops, or enhancing the seasoning with a secret dash of Worcestershire sauce or other seasoning.

SPECIES
Sui generis.

RADISH
CAKES

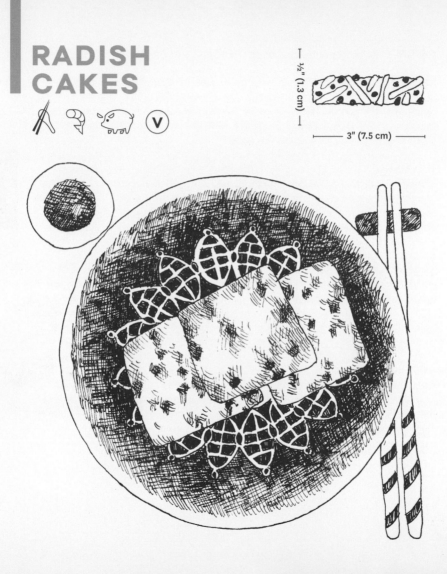

½" (1.3 cm)

3" (7.5 cm)

GENUS 蘿蔔糕 · *luóbó gāo* · *lo⁴ baak⁶ gou¹*

IDENTIFICATION Large, mild Chinese radishes are grated and mixed with rice flour into a thin batter, steamed in a large mold, and then cut into ½-inch (1.3-cm) slices and pan-fried without a batter until crisp. Both the radish and the rice flour are very mild, so savory little chunks of *lop chong*, black mushrooms, dried shrimp, fried shallots, and Chinese ham are often added.

The best radish cakes are served fresh off the grill. Some teahouses cut the cakes into cubes which are then deep-fried; this interpretation triples the crunchy surface and turns them even crustier. Other places occasionally offer simple slices of the steamed cakes. Exterior is crusty and browned; interior is creamy and usually studded with chewy nuggets. Sometimes called 菜頭粿 · *càitóu guǒ* · *coi³ tau⁴ gwo²* ("radish rice cake") in Southern dialects.

BASIC FILLING
In addition to the shredded radishes and rice flour batter, a good handful of finely chopped savory ingredients is usually added.

DEFAULT SAUCE OR DIP
Red vinegar sometimes seasoned with soy sauce and/or garlic.

NESTING HABITS
Served as crispy slices or cubes on a plate with the sauce on the side.

ORIGINS
Most likely developed out of a much plainer New Year dish still popular in Hakka areas, Chaozhou, and Southern Fujian—as well as in Southeast Asia—that is basically rice flour mixed into a batter and steamed. At home, these slices are often pan-fried with eggs into an omelet sprinkled with fried peanuts, chopped salted radish, green onion, and cilantro.

SPECIES
- **Taro Cakes**
  芋頭糕
  yùtóu gāo · *wu⁶ tau⁴ gou¹*
  Small cubes and the mashed paste of mature taro are added to the rice batter instead of the shredded radish.

SHREDDED LOTUS FRITTERS

½" (1.2 cm)

2" (5 cm)

GENUS 香煎蓮藕餅 · *xiāngjiān liánǒu bǐng* · *hoeng¹ zin¹ lin⁴ ngau⁵ beng²*

IDENTIFICATION These crunchy patties are celebrations of the deliciously sweet roots of the lotus, and so are at their best in the autumn when they have just been harvested out of deep layers of cold mud. These ivory rhizomes are shredded or even finely diced, seasoned, bound with beaten eggs and a slurry made out of cornstarch or something similar, and then pan-fried into golden cakes. In spite of all of this attention, the sweet, crisp lotus root retains its texture and flavor.

Because the main ingredient is so mild, aromatics are generally kept to a bare minimum. While some places offer this as an exercise in restraint, most teahouses will toss in a bit of ground pork or fish paste, or maybe some tiny morsels of *lop chong* and dried shrimp, to add other layers of flavor. Exterior is crunchy and golden; interior is soft and sweet.

BASIC FILLING
Lotus roots are cut into dainty pieces and bound with eggs and rice flour, along with seasonings and nuggets of savory ingredients.

DEFAULT SAUCE OR DIP
Usually accompanied by a dry-fried salt and pepper dip.

NESTING HABITS
Three or so patties are arrayed on a small plate, often on a bed of finely shredded cabbage or lettuce to wick away the oil.

ORIGINS
Undoubtedly introduced to Guangdong from the Yangtze River Valley, these have been enthusiastically adopted in the wetter parts of Guangdong. The Stuffed Lotus Sandwiches (below) sometimes are given fish paste fillings in the style of the Pearl River Delta.

SPECIES
• **Stuffed Lotus Sandwiches**
  蓮藕餅
  liánǒu bǐng · *lin⁴ ngau⁵ beng²*
  This specialty from northern Hubei along the Yangtze River sandwiches fresh pork forcemeat between thin slices of fresh lotus root that are then dusted with starch and pan-fried until golden.

GARLIC CHIVE PACKETS

1" (2.5 cm)

1" (2.5 cm)

GENUS 煎韭菜粿 · *jiān jiǔcài guǒ* · *zin¹ gau² coi³ gwo²*

IDENTIFICATION Translucent balls stuffed with finely chopped garlic chives and the occasional fresh shrimp are pan-fried on both sides to create a light golden crust. The Chinese variety of chives is flat and much wider than its Western counterpart, is much more like a true vegetable, and possesses the warm aroma of fresh garlic. The wrappers are made out of sweet potato flour and wheat starch mixed with boiling water, and this gives the packets a snappy texture.

Sweet potato flour is a signature ingredient of a delectable trifecta in China's cuisines: the region surrounding the southern edge of Fujian, northeastern Guangdong, and the inland hill country. This is where the foods of Chaozhou, the Hakka, and Southern Fujian have intertwined for centuries. Exterior is dry and tacky, with the fried areas slightly crisp; interior is juicy and very flavorful.

BASIC FILLING
Chopped garlic chives seasoned with salt, pepper, and a touch of oil to provide a buttery texture against the stark cleanliness of the vegetable. Diced fresh shrimp are often added to create a sweet, pink contrast to the aromatic, emerald chives.

DEFAULT SAUCE OR DIP
None.

NESTING HABITS
Three on a plate, often arranged on a doily or shredded lettuce.

ORIGINS
Garlic chive packets are members of the enormous group of steamed or pan-fried foods called *guo* that are popular throughout Southern Fujian, Hakka areas, Chaozhou, and wherever the Chinese diaspora has set down roots, such as in many parts of Southeast Asia. *Guo* are also made from ground sticky rice, or sometimes from wheat starch (see Fun Gor, page 32), and may be filled.

SPECIES
- **Steamed Garlic Chive Packets**
  韭菜粿
  jiǔcài guǒ · *gau² coi³ gwo²*
  These are exactly the same as the main genus, except that they are steamed.

HONEYCOMB TARO-WRAPPED PORK

1½" (3.8 cm)

1½" (3.8 cm)

GENUS 蜂巢炸芋角 · *fēngcháo zhá yù jiǎo* · *fung¹ caau⁴ zaa³ wu⁶ gok³*

IDENTIFICATION Football-shaped, with a golden, brittle, webbed exterior that becomes soft and pasty toward the center, these fried dim sum possess meaty insides bound with a light gravy. Mashed taro is combined with wheat starch and lard, and this explodes in the hot oil to form the distinctive nets of golden thread that cover its surface, what the Chinese describe as a "honeycomb." Underneath this crunchy mesh lies a layer of the faintly purplish taro that cradles a rough, gravelly mixture of ground pork and other savory ingredients.

Absolutely at their best when freshly fried, these must be eaten hot or at least very warm in order to enjoy their textures to the fullest. They are clipped open as they are served. Exterior is crunchy and then creamy; interior is pebbly with a light gravy.

BASIC FILLING
Ground pork is the main ingredient for the filling, although fresh shrimp, *char siu*, black mushrooms, and other savory items may be added.

DEFAULT SAUCE OR DIP
Mix together mustard and soy sauce.

NESTING HABITS
Three nest together on a single plate inside of little cupcake liners or on a paper doily to soak up any extra oil.

ORIGINS
Now found in most Cantonese-style teahouses and dim sum parlors, these probably originated in Guangxi, the subtropical province that lies just to the west of Guangdong. Some of the best quality taro are grown in Lipu near scenic Guilin, which is why these are sometimes referred to as "Lipu taro-wrapped pork" in Chinese.

SPECIES
- **Five-Spice Taro Jiaozi**
  五香芋蓉餃
  wǔxiāng yùróng jiǎo ·
  ng⁵ hoeng¹ wu⁶ jung⁴ gaau²
  The crispy crust of honeycomb taro-wrapped pork is not found in any other variety of dim sum, but this steamed species morphs that exterior into a creamy filling and traps it inside a translucent Fun Gor–type (page 32) wrapper.

COFFEE
PORK RIBS

1" (2.5 cm)

1" (2.5 cm)

GENUS 咖啡排骨 · *kāfēi páigú* · *gaa³ fe¹ paai⁴ gwat¹*

IDENTIFICATION Marinated ribs are coated in an egg batter, fried until very crispy, and then quickly chucked into a syrupy mixture of strong coffee, sugar, and soy sauce. This thick, sweetened coffee syrup forms a deliciously brittle surface once the sugar hits the cool air. The ribs may be crosscut into bite-size pieces or left as long bones; in either case, they encourage extended nibbling in order to gnaw out every last morsel of flavorful meat, chewy tendon, and glassy crust.

At their best when just out of the fryer, the ribs feature gentle bitterness of the coffee, sweetness of the sugar, and savoriness of the soy sauce, making a satisfying range of flavors against the mouthwatering pork. Exterior is glazed and crunchy; interior is meaty and juicy.

DEFAULT SAUCE OR DIP
Sometimes has a dollop of sweetened whipped cream on the side to enhance the coffee notes and make this seem like an extraordinarily hedonistic take on Viennese *Kaffee mit Schlag*.

NESTING HABITS
A doily or lettuce leaf is sometimes called upon to disguise any oil.

ORIGINS
Most definitely a brainchild of Hong Kong's creative chefs, this unique dish weds the iconic Chinese dish of spareribs with an unmistakably Western flavor: coffee. This is a relatively new genus in the large family of fried pork dishes, and its combination of dark coffee with sugar and soy sauce is now sometimes used to season other rich dark meats, like duck and goose, although pork ribs remain the hands-down favorite.

SPECIES
- **Coffee Chicken Wings**
  咖啡雞翅
  kāfēi jīchì · *gaa³ fe¹ gai¹ ci³*
  Sectioned chicken wings are braised in a similar sauce, but usually are not deep-fried first.

FRIED RICE-DOUGH PACKETS

1½" (3.8 cm)

1½" (3.8 cm)

GENUS 鹽水餃 · *yánshuǐ jiǎo* · *jim⁴ seoi² gaau²*

IDENTIFICATION These slightly elongated ovals have a pale gold exterior with a rough and sandy feel. Just under the surface, the gently crispy crust yields to a layer of lightly sweetened sticky rice paste that fries up into a puffed-up balloon sporting gentle points at each end, while inside is a gravelly mixture of deeply savory ingredients like *char siu*, chopped dried crustaceans, chicken, and black mushrooms in a light gravy.

These are cut in half as they are served, which allows visual appreciation of the tumble of delectable multicolored pebbles inside a thin, chewy bubble. Exterior possesses an initial feeling of sandpaper that dissolves into a soft, gummy layer; interior is a satisfying little mouthful of tensile savory bits.

BASIC FILLING
A loose mixture of meats, dried shrimp, and savory vegetables bound together in a light sauce.

DEFAULT SAUCE OR DIP
None necessary, but soy sauce can be mixed with mustard, if desired.

NESTING HABITS
These cluster together in groups of three or so on a plate with a paper doily underneath to collect the oil.

ORIGINS
A permanent member of most teahouse dim sum offerings, fried rice-dough packets definitely hail from Guangdong province, although the exact location is subject to debate. One very good possibility is that these originally came from the northeastern edge of the province near Chaozhou, where the contrast of sweet rice paste with a savory filling is a very common delight. Fried rice-dough packets thus display one of the interesting hallmarks of southern coastal China's snacks: the contrast of sweet and savory in a single dish. Sweets—especially in Chaozhou—are not relegated to the dessert table, but often are included as part of the main entrées.

SPECIES
Sui generis.

SOY SKIN
ROLLS

1½" (3.8 cm)

1½" (3.8 cm)

GENUS 腐皮卷 · *fǔpí juǎn* · *fu⁶ pei⁴ gyun²*

IDENTIFICATION With their blistered golden exterior and a juicy filling of shredded vegetables, these rolls can be either completely meatless or include other proteins. Thin sheets of soy skin (also known by their Japanese name, *yuba*) enclose the filling in what looks much like a Spring Roll (page 92), which is then fried to make the outer layer bubble and crisp up, while the inner layers of soy skin remain soft and pliable.

Indisputably best when very hot and then snipped in half just as they are served, these still retain their charm after they cool off a bit. Exterior has a crunchy layer over a thicker soft one that is slightly chewy; interior is mildly tensile with shredded vegetables and the occasional protein.

BASIC FILLING
Thin ribbons of vegetables such as carrots, radish, bamboo shoots, garlic chives, wood ear fungus, and mung bean sprouts are the main ingredients. The filling may be vegetarian, pork, fresh shrimp, or chicken, seasoned with ginger, green onions, cilantro, and/or garlic.

DEFAULT SAUCE OR DIP
A salt-and-pepper or soy sauce–based dip, or a small bowl of mayonnaise.

NESTING HABITS
Two or three rolls cuddle together on a plate, often atop a paper doily or shredded cabbage.

ORIGINS
Ostensibly from Guangdong and popular throughout Hong Kong, these are dead ringers for the Yangtze River Valley dish called "vegetarian goose." Recipes for classic East China dishes such as this most likely were carried with the diaspora that sent waves of settlers south into Guangdong many centuries ago.

SPECIES
• **Steamed Soy Skin Rolls**
蒸腐皮捲
zhēng fǔpí juǎn · *zing¹ fu⁶ pei⁴ gyun²*
Identical to regular soy skin rolls, except that they have been doused with a savory sauce seasoned mainly by soy sauce and then steamed until soft.

SPRING
ROLLS

¾" (1.9 cm)

1" (2.5 cm)

GENUS 春卷 · *chūnjuǎn* · *ceon¹ gyun²*

IDENTIFICATION Extremely thin pasta sheets are wrapped around a shredded filling and deep-fried until crispy and golden brown. These wheat pasta rounds can be made commercially, put together from a high-gluten batter, or formed in the traditional manner by dabbing a large ball of fresh gluten on a hot griddle until its surface is barely covered with an instantly cooked, fine web of crispy pasta.

No matter how the wrappers are made, the main ingredients in spring rolls are mung bean sprouts and finely shredded vegetables. These are rolled into cigars, deep-fried until golden, and then clipped open when served. Exterior is crunchy and flaky; interior is juicy and full of barely cooked vegetables and the occasional protein. Sometimes referred to in English as "egg rolls."

BASIC FILLING
Bean sprouts mixed with thin shreds of cabbage, carrots, bamboo shoots, cellophane noodles, and mushrooms or wood ears bound with a seasoned light gravy; can include finely chopped pork or shrimp.

DEFAULT SAUCE OR DIP
Worcestershire sauce; sweet-and-sour sauce is often proffered at more Anglicized restaurants.

NESTING HABITS
Three rolls gathered on a doily centered on a small plate.

ORIGINS
Popular throughout much of South China, spring rolls got their name because they are traditionally made for the Chinese New Year, which is also called the Spring Festival in Chinese. They were mentioned in such works as the thirteenth-century work on folk customs called 歲時廣記 · *Suìshí guǎngjì.*

SPECIES
- **Fried Wontons**
  炸雲吞
  zhá yúntūn · *zaa³ wan⁴ tan¹*
  Very thin 2-inch (5-cm) pasta squares are stuffed with finely chopped pork, shrimp, vegetables or other fillings, folded into packets, and deep-fried.

PAPER-WRAPPED CHICKEN

3" (7.5 cm)

GENUS 紙包雞 · *zhǐ bāo jī* · *zi² baau¹ gai¹*

IDENTIFICATION Bite-size chunks of chicken marinated in a highly seasoned sauce are enclosed in small packets of thin paper or foil and then deep-fried. Although they are customarily wrapped in paper, dim sum restaurants nowadays tend to use foil instead, which makes wrapping easier and the packets a whole lot tidier. The paper or foil protects the tender chicken from the high heat of a deep fryer, allowing it to cook quickly without drying out. Warm aromatics like five-spice powder or citrusy notes from cured tangerine peel or deep savory notes courtesy of fermented black beans add considerable zip to the relatively neutral background of the chicken, which is tinted a dark brown from the layer of thick soy sauce.

A packet may contain three or four chunks of bone-in chicken, as well as a good dollop of sauce to keep things moist and sticky. The diner extracts the contents of each packet on his or her own and nibbles on each luscious piece without feeling the necessity for sharing. Exterior is inedible paper or foil; interior contains juicy chunks of chicken on the bone with a dark, aromatic sauce.

PAN- AND
DEEP-FRIED

BASIC FILLING
Tender pieces of dark meat—usually with the bones still inside—are jumbled in a vibrant sauce that often contains fermented black beans, ginger, garlic, sand ginger, or cured tangerine peel; might have oyster sauce in there, too.

DEFAULT SAUCE OR DIP
None.

NESTING HABITS
Six or so unhatched packets nestled on a plate.

ORIGINS
Different areas of China have their own recipes for paper-wrapped chicken, but the most famous comes from Wuzhou in Guangxi, which lies just to the west of Guangdong. It is one of Guangxi's most well-known dishes, and the combination of powerful seasonings blasted this way into the tender chicken has caused it to spread far beyond its natural habitat.

SPECIES
Sui generis.

WRAPPED CRAB CLAWS

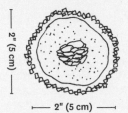

2" (5 cm)

2" (5 cm)

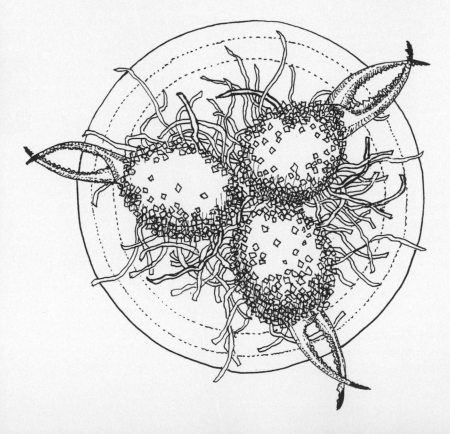

GENUS 釀蟹鉗 · *niàng xièqián* · *joeng⁶ haai⁵ kim⁴*

IDENTIFICATION These beautiful dim sum are easily identified by the long crab pinchers that stick out at one end and act as convenient handles for snapping them up with the fingers. The outer shell of a crab claw is removed, leaving only the pinchers intact. Shrimp or crab forcemeat covers the meaty part of the claw and forms a ball, which is then rolled in a double-bound coating (cornstarch, egg wash, then bread crumbs) before being deep-fried. Absolutely breathtaking when fresh out of the fryer. Exterior is crunchy and dry; the interior is initially soft and juicy before yielding to the sweet and succulent crabmeat. Sometimes referred to in English as "stuffed crab claw," a direct (but misleading) translation.

BASIC FILLING
Chopped fresh shrimp mixed with either pork or crab (or sometimes just shrimp) is lightly seasoned with ginger, green onion, and rice wine.

DEFAULT SAUCE OR DIP
A saucer of mayonnaise, soy sauce, or sweet-and-sour sauce may be offered on the side.

NESTING HABITS
These congregate in groups of three or four on a plate, usually with their bottoms touching and the claws arrayed toward the outside. Shredded lettuce or a doily may be provided to wick away any extra oil.

ORIGINS
Most likely first created in Guangzhou as a fancy banquet dish. Swankier teahouses in Hong Kong and elsewhere have enthusiastically adopted these as part of their regular repertoire. A chef probably developed these out of traditional shrimp balls (page 101), which have been part of Guangzhou's dim sum repertoire for a very long time.

SPECIES
- **Steamed Wrapped Crab Claws**
  蒸釀蟹鉗
  zhēng niàng xièqián · *zing¹ joeng⁶ haai⁵ kim⁴*
  Here the forcemeat is not breaded, but rather the wrapped claws are placed on a plate and steamed, which creates a tasty sauce. As a result, these are much softer and juicier than the fried version.

DEEP-FRIED SHRIMP POUCHES

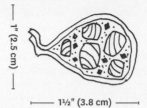

1" (2.5 cm)

1½" (3.8 cm)

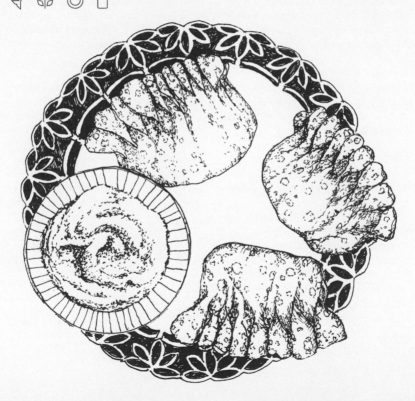

GENUS 沙律明蝦角 · *shālù míngxiā jiǎo* · *saa¹ leot² ming⁴ haa¹ gok³*

IDENTIFICATION Thin pasta wrappers form fat purses around chopped fresh shrimp that are then deep-fried to a golden brown. These are best made with wonton skins or spring roll wrappers so that tiny bubbles form on the outside and make this super crunchy. The edges are highly frilled in contrast with the smooth belly.

A relatively new member of the dim sum family, these can be considered one of the more luxurious teahouse offerings, as they are celebrations of hedonistic textures and flavors: the fresh sweetness of excellent shrimp is complemented by tiny bits of vegetal crunch bound with a silky white sauce of sweetened milk or mayo, and given a brittle shell that emphasizes all of these contrasts. Exterior is highly crispy, especially along the frills; interior is lush, naturally sweet, and juicy.

BASIC FILLING
Fresh shrimp—often whole pieces mixed with chopped— provide textural interest and explosions of honeyed juiciness. Scallops are sometimes also included and are excellent whenever they appear in this supporting role. Mainly seasoned with sweetened condensed milk and mayonnaise, though tiny bits of crisp vegetables like Chinese celery or bamboo shoots may dot the interior.

DEFAULT SAUCE OR DIP
Mayonnaise, which is the "salad" (that is, salad dressing) in the Chinese name, as noted in this dish's Cantonese pronunciation: *saa¹ leot²*.

NESTING HABITS
Three plump purses are usually huddled together on a doily with a small bowl of mayo.

ORIGINS
These were most likely a 1980s invention in Hong Kong and are a cross-cultural riff that combines a Cantonese classic—Har Gow (page 34)—with English prawn sandwiches.

SPECIES
• **Deep-Fried Lobster Jiaozi**
  沙律龍蝦角
  shālù lóngxiā jiǎo · *saa¹ leot² lung⁴ haa¹ gok³*
  Chunks of fresh lobster take the place of shrimp in this sumptuous spin-off.

CROUTON
SHRIMP BALLS

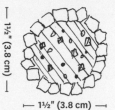

1½" (3.8 cm)

1½" (3.8 cm)

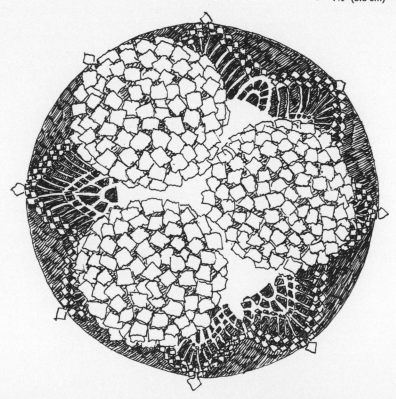

GENUS 金黃炸蝦球 · *jīnhuáng zhá xiā qíu* · *gam¹ wong⁴ zaa³ haa¹ kau⁴*

IDENTIFICATION These charming golden nuggets have tiny bread cubes stuck all over the surface. The outside is then fried to a crisp, while the interior turns into a luscious ball of fresh shrimp that is both bouncy and bright pink. The bread cubes become ethereally light when done correctly and provide a sensuous crunch that then yields to the hot juices in the center. See if these can be fried to order, which is when they are at their absolute best. Exterior is crispy and light; interior is dense and juicy.

BASIC FILLING
Generally minced fresh shrimp combined with fresh pork fat for extra juiciness and such ingredients as crunchy water chestnuts, ginger, and green onion.

DEFAULT SAUCE OR DIP
Mayonnaise, ketchup, or some other simple dip.

NESTING HABITS
Three to five on a plate, often nestled on a paper doily.

ORIGINS
Yet another classic dim sum offering that on the surface seems to be Cantonese through and through, this actually might be a variation on the Shandong appetizer called "shrimp toasts," which, like crouton shrimp balls, feature seasoned fresh minced shrimp paired with Western-style fried bread; the main difference is that in North China this forcemeat is spread on squares of white bread before each tidbit is deep-fried.

SPECIES

- **Frizzy Shrimp Balls**
  金絲百花球
  jīnsī bǎihuā qiú · *gam¹ si¹ baak³ faa¹ kau⁴*
  The shrimp forcemeat is swaddled in shredded wonton skins or wrapped with something like Middle Eastern *kataifi* (shredded phyllo dough) before being fried to a golden brown.

- **Fried Shrimp Balls**
  炸蝦球
  zhá xiā qíu · *zaa³ haa¹ kau⁴*
  These are not encrusted in any way, shape, or form, but are directly fried in hot oil until they puff up and look tanned. Sometimes a small whole shrimp is enclosed in the forcemeat, its existence announced by the tail sticking out of the top.

SINGAPORE RICE NOODLES

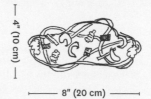

4" (10 cm)

8" (20 cm)

GENUS 星洲炒米粉 · *Xīngzhōu chǎo mǐfěn* · *Sing¹ zau¹ caau² mai⁵ fan²*

IDENTIFICATION Thin rice vermicelli are stir-fried in a light curry sauce with shreds of *char siu*, sweet peppers, bean sprouts, chicken, eggs, onions, and shrimp. The noodles soak up most of the sauce and so act as a tasty backdrop for the flavors and textures of the contrasting meats and vegetables, which are usually added at the last minute to retain their individuality.

Of all Chinese pasta dishes, Singapore rice noodles have the most powdery texture on the tongue thanks to the curry powder, but this ends up adding to its allure. These are almost always specially ordered off the menu. The noodles are a combination of snappy and soft thin threads; the meats are slightly chewy, and both the shrimp and the vegetables are crisp.

DEFAULT SAUCE OR DIP
Mustard mixed with soy sauce as a dip, if you are so inclined.

NESTING HABITS
Loops and swirls of rice noodles nestle down in the plate, with the larger ingredients either perched on top or burrowed inside; often available in Chinese delis.

ORIGINS
This is a matter of debate. Some say that this dish arrived in Hong Kong after being invented in Singapore, but others insist that it was created in Hong Kong and had the name "Singapore" slapped on it thanks to the curry powder in the mix. In the end, it does not really matter, as this delectable tangle of noodles has distinct Hong Kong flavors and textures, thanks to the abundant shrimp and *char siu*.

SPECIES
Sui generis. Other areas of South China offer variations on fried rice noodles, but Singapore rice noodles is the main contribution from Hong Kong to this family.

CHOW FUN

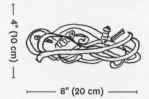

4" (10 cm)

8" (20 cm)

GENUS 炒河粉 · *chǎo héfěn* · *caau² ho⁴ fan²*

IDENTIFICATION Rice noodles about ½ inch (1.1 cm) wide are stir-fried with meats and vegetables. When made correctly, the soy sauce that coats and seasons the noodles is seared and browned in lots of oil, making the edges slightly chewy, while the noodles themselves remain loose and light. This oil is then poured off before the noodles are tossed with stir-fried meats and barely crisp vegetables.

Favorite accompaniments are thin slices of steak, halved fresh shrimp, vegetarian combinations, or slivers of pork with lots of mung bean sprouts and green onions. Rice noodles like these are always best made to order. Noodles will have browned edges with soft interiors; the vegetables are always crunchy, while the proteins will provide chewy or crisp notes.

DEFAULT SAUCE OR DIP
Pan juices from the meats seasoned with soy sauce and other condiments.

NESTING HABITS
Slithery browned noodles coil around the other ingredients on a lipped plate; often available in Chinese delis.

ORIGINS
Cantonese rice noodles are called 沙河粉 · *Shāhé fěn* · *Saa¹ ho⁴ fan²* in Chinese because their place of origin is generally agreed to be the village of Shahe just to the north of Guangzhou. It is believed to have been invented there some time around 1860, and one of the legends that surround its creation says it came about after the proprietors of a small mom-and-pop eatery in the village fed a starving old man. The male owner later fell deathly ill, and the person they had saved created a dish of fresh rice noodles to revive his appetite. It turned out that this old man was an imperial chef banished from the palace after displeasing the Dowager Empress Cixi.

SPECIES
• **Thick Rice Noodles**
貴刁 or 粿條
guìdiāo · *gwai³ diu¹* or *guǒtiáo* · *gwo² tiu⁴*
A heftier rice noodle from the Chaozhou area of northeastern Guangdong, these are usually stir-fried or served in soups.

FRIED RICE

4" (10 cm)

8" (20 cm)

GENUS 炒飯 · *chǎofàn* · *caau² fan⁶*

IDENTIFICATION Cold, cooked rice is stir-fried with bits of meat, poultry, seafood, eggs, and/or vegetables to form a hot, savory pile of distinct, seasoned grains. The key to great fried rice is excellent quality grains that are steamed and then completely cooled before they are stir-fried, as this prevents the starchy coating from forming thick clumps. Chinese chefs rarely season their fried rice with soy sauce—and if they do, it is with a very light touch—so that the sweetness of the rice and the individual flavors of the condiments shine through. This should always be made to order, and it is quite all right to eat this with a spoon if you're not at a fancy banquet. The rice consists of gently chewy, distinct grains; the other ingredients are small and can be crispy or chewy or soft.

DEFAULT SAUCE OR DIP
None.

NESTING HABITS
Tumbled up in a loose pile on a rimmed plate or platter; often available in Chinese delis.

ORIGINS
It is believed that Cantonese fried rice originated in the culinary capital of Yangzhou (see the second species at right), which lies in Jiangsu to the north of Shanghai. Over one thousand years ago, Xie Feng mentioned something quite similar in the 食經 · *Shí jīng* (*Dining Classic*) and called it "broken gold rice," presumably after the scrambled eggs. Today in Yangzhou, this dish also includes

more extravagant items such as sea cucumbers, shrimp roe, scallops, and Shaoxing rice wine.

SPECIES
- **Fried Rice with Chicken and Salted Fish**
  鹹魚雞粒炒飯
  xiányú jīlì chǎofàn ·
  haam⁴ jyu⁴ gai¹ lap¹ caau² fan⁶
  Bits of salted fish provide a delicious funkiness in contrast with the fresh, diced chicken; shredded lettuce often rounds out and lightens the mix.

- **Yangzhou Fried Rice**
  揚州炒飯
  Yángzhōu chǎofàn · *Joeng⁴ zau¹ caau² fan⁶*
  The rice is tossed with scrambled eggs, fresh shrimp, and bits of *char siu* or Chinese ham, and salt.

CONGEE

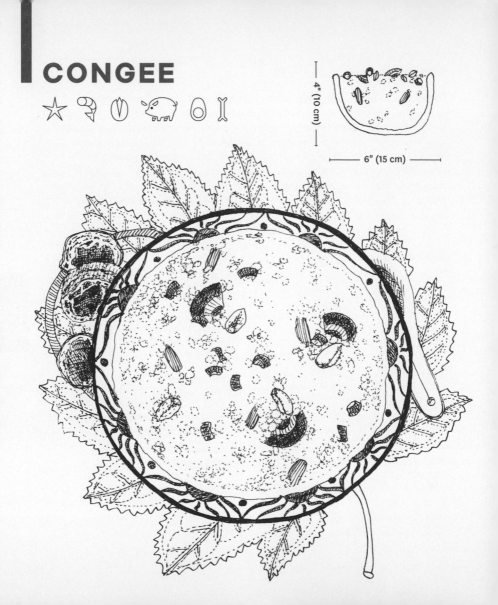

4" (10 cm)

6" (15 cm)

GENUS 粥 · *zhōu* · *zuk¹*

IDENTIFICATION Regular rice is cooked in a large amount of water or stock until the grains thicken into a loose porridge. Congee is usually unseasoned until the cook adds whatever condiments are required.

Good Chinese delis offer the greatest variety of congees. Many are exercises in smooth textures, others offer an array of chewy and crunchy bits, and a few concentrate all of the attention on the rice itself. The creamy hot rice porridge is usually interspersed with savory ingredients to supply flavorful and textural contrasts, and it often has a cilantro or green onion garnish.

DEFAULT SAUCE OR DIP
Soy sauce for the possible side of sliced cruller.

NESTING HABITS
Generally nestles in a large bowl, sometimes with toasty slices of Chinese cruller on the side, which are to be dipped in soy sauce between sips of the porridge for salty, crunch-filled punches that clear the palate.

ORIGINS
Guangzhou is generally acknowledged as the home of congee, but variations on this delicious theme can be found throughout Southern Fujian, Chaozhou, Hong Kong, and other places in South China.

SPECIES
- **Pork and Preserved Egg Congee**
  皮蛋瘦肉粥
  pídàn shòuròu zhōu •
  pei⁴ daan⁶ sau³ juk⁶ zuk¹
  Lean pork and wedges of black preserved eggs are added to the hot congee; peanuts and green onions decorate the top.

- **Sampan Congee**
  艇仔粥
  tǐngzǐ zhōu • *teng⁵ zai² zuk¹*
  Delicious kitchen sink mixture of squid, porky odds and ends, shrimp, peanuts, green onions, and whatever else the cook likes. Was once sold by hawkers on sampans, hence its name.

- **Roast Duck Congee**
  烤鸭粥
  kǎo yā zhōu • *haau¹ ngaap³ zuk¹*
  Chopped duck with the bones plus its juices and a dusting of cilantro.

EXTRAS

LO MEIN

4" (10 cm)

8" (20 cm)

GENUS 撈麵 · *lāomiàn* · *laau⁴ min⁶*

IDENTIFICATION Cooked egg pasta is tossed with a sauce, condiments, and other ingredients, like vegetables and shrimp roe. Thin noodles are generally used for lo mein, and the preferred seasoning is oyster sauce. Cantonese egg noodles are often a bright yellow to signify the presence of the eggs and alkali (such as baking soda), which give them a particularly bouncy character.

Lo mein is always made to order. These noodles are blanched very quickly in order to preserve their special texture. The noodles are therefore very tensile and smooth, the sauce is thick and clings to each strand, and the other ingredients retain their individual textures and flavors.

DEFAULT SAUCE OR DIP
Oyster sauce is usually preferred unless it conflicts with the flavor of the proteins.

NESTING HABITS
A fluffy pile on a rimmed plate with the condiments prominently displayed; often available in Chinese delis.

ORIGINS
Tossed noodles are popular throughout most of China. These usually are eaten as a snack or quick meal, and so they might appear as fully balanced meals with meat and vegetables, or else turn up as simple concoctions that are meant to deliver more in the way of arresting flavor than nutrition. At a dim sum meal, these and most other noodle dishes would therefore be side attractions designed to bolster the other foods that crowd the table toward the end of the meal.

SPECIES
- **Green Onion and Ginger Lo Mein**
  蔥薑撈麵
  cōng jiāng lāomiàn · *cung¹ goeng¹ laau⁴ min⁶*
  A simple mixture of noodles and oyster sauce tossed with shredded raw green onions and ginger.

- **Shrimp Roe Lo Mein**
  蝦籽撈麵
  xiāzi lāomiàn · *haa¹ zi² laau⁴ min⁶*
  Dried shrimp roe is lightly fried and sprinkled over the seasoned lo mein noodles; if you are lucky, the noodles will also include the shrimp roe in the dough.

CRISPY
NOODLE
PILLOW

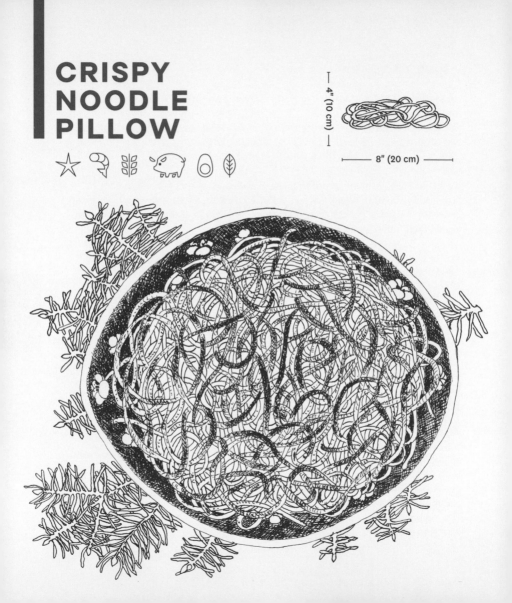

4" (10 cm)

8" (20 cm)

GENUS 兩面黃 · *liángmiàn huáng* · *loeng⁵ min⁶ wong⁴*

IDENTIFICATION Handfuls of cooked egg noodles are tossed in oil and slowly pan-fried until the bottom is a golden brown before the thick pillow is turned over and fried on the other side.

The dish is always made to order, and the seasonings and condiments vary according to the cook and the style of restaurant, but no matter what is used, the star of the show is that big, golden nest of pasta. Any toppings are placed on the pillow just before serving, and then the diners break up the crust and toss the strands with the gravy. The noodle pillow has a crunchy, crispy exterior and a soft, luscious interior.

DEFAULT SAUCE OR DIP
Often oyster sauce, but this can vary so that the sauce acts as a perfect foil for the other ingredients.

NESTING HABITS
A large, proud, golden cushion of pasta rests on a lipped plate with the supporting cast balanced on top.

ORIGINS
Most likely an immigrant from the lower Yangtze River area, where this sort of crispy pasta is still spotted in large numbers. Even today, the seasonings, ingredients, and textures of the two species are so similar that they are at times virtually indistinguishable.

SPECIES
- **Shrimp Crispy Noodle Pillow**
  蝦仁兩面黃
  xiārén liángmiàn huáng ·
  haa¹ jan⁴ loeng⁵ min⁶ wong⁴
  Fresh whole shrimp are stir-fried with bok choy and finished with a pale gravy.

- **Shredded Pork Crispy Noodle Pillow**
  肉絲兩面黃
  ròusī liángmiàn huáng ·
  juk⁶ si¹ loeng⁵ min⁶ wong⁴
  Thin strips of lean pork are stir-fried with assorted vegetables, and then a lightly thickened sauce seasoned with soy sauce binds them together.

GAI LAN WITH OYSTER SAUCE

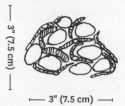

3" (7.5 cm)

3" (7.5 cm)

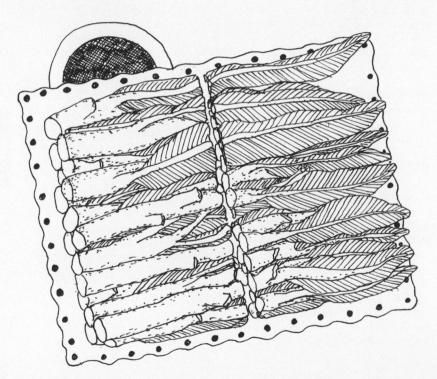

GENUS 蠔油芥藍 · *háoyóu jièlán* · *ci³ jau⁴ gaai³ laam⁴*

IDENTIFICATION Young tips of Chinese flowering kale are blanched and then coated with oyster sauce—or given a small saucer as a dip—when they are served to preserve their beautiful emerald color. The flowers on these tender shoots should still be unopened buds, which ensures their sublime texture.

This is one of the very few vegetables to be paraded around a dim sum teahouse, perhaps because it tastes delicious hot or at room temperature, and its texture does not suffer, either. Just before serving, the whole stack is snipped in half. The vegetable stems are crisp and sweet, the leaves are soft and silky, and the sauce provides a savory note with a hint of the sea. Sometimes called "Chinese broccoli."

DEFAULT SAUCE OR DIP
Oyster sauce.

NESTING HABITS
Always appears on a rimmed oval plate as a tidy pile with the stems at one end and the leaves at the other; often available in Chinese delis.

ORIGINS
This dish most likely was created in Hong Kong, as oyster sauce was an invention of the founder of Lee Kum Kee and first marketed in 1888. True oyster sauce is rich and has a caramelized edge, as well as the underlying aroma of shellfish. Gai lan is popular in Guangdong and throughout Southeast Asia, where warm weather and ample water allows it to grow rapidly into tender shoots.

SPECIES
- **Stir-Fried Gai Lan with Garlic**
  蒜蓉炒芥藍
  suànróng chǎo jièlán ·
  syun³ jung⁴ caau² gaai³ laam⁴
  The kale is cut on a deep diagonal and then stir-fried with oil, salt, and chopped garlic; made to order.

- **Garlic Romaine Lettuce**
  蒜子羅曼生菜
  suànzi luómàn shēngcài ·
  syun³ zi⁹ lo⁴ maan⁶ saang¹ coi³
  Whole long leaves of crispy lettuce are blanched and then topped with stir-fried pork and chiles seasoned with lots of garlic and a splash of soy sauce; made to order.

STIR-FRIED WATER SPINACH WITH BEAN CURD CHEESE

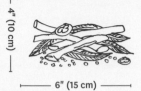

4" (10 cm)

6" (15 cm)

☆ 🌶 Ⓥ

GENUS 腐乳蕹菜 • *fŭrŭ yōngcài* • *fu⁶ jyu⁵ jung¹ coi³*

IDENTIFICATION Water spinach is a type of morning glory that grows especially well in the tropics. Its stems are shaped like straws, which is why the Chinese also call it "hollow vegetable" (空心菜 • *kōngxīncài* • *hung¹ sam¹ coi³*), among many other names. The leaves are long and shaped like arrowheads, and their taste is very similar to that of spinach. The stems, though, have a slightly nutty taste and offer crisp contrast to the soft leaves.

Water spinach is almost always cut into 2-inch (5-cm) lengths and stir-fried. In this dish, a type of Chinese fermented bean curd cheese adds a creamy yet funky edge, and it is usually punctuated with thin slices of fresh green chiles. This dish is almost always made to order. The leaves are silky and dark green, the stems are crisp and pale green, and these are coated in a thin, creamy sauce. Sometimes called "Chinese spinach" or "ong choy" in English; in Chinese it is also known as 通菜 • *tōngcài* • *tong¹ coi³*.

DEFAULT SAUCE OR DIP
Mashed fermented bean curd cheese tossed with green chiles and mild rice wine.

NESTING HABITS
A tangle of stems and leaves nestle on a rimmed plate.

ORIGINS
Water spinach is very popular throughout tropical Asia, so knowledge of where it was first cultivated has been lost in the mists of time. Fermented bean curd cheese, though, is very Chinese and is a creamy ingredient brined much like feta cheese. This has been used in China for at least two thousand years. Mainly beloved in South China, it can be white, yellow, or red, and the seasonings range from a slightly sweet edge to extremely funky to decidedly hot, depending upon the seasonings.

SPECIES
• **Water Spinach Stir-Fried with Garlic**
  蒜蓉炒蕹菜
  suànróng chǎo yōngcài •
  syun³ jung⁴ caau² jung¹ coi³
  A handful of freshly chopped garlic and salt season the otherwise plain stir-fried vegetables.

SWEET
DIM SUM

FRIED SESAME
BALLS

2" (5 cm)

2" (5 cm)

GENUS 煎堆 · *jiānduī* · *zin¹ deoi¹*

IDENTIFICATION Round rice-dough balloons completely covered with toasted sesame seeds have a smidgen of sweet red bean paste inside. The wrappers possess an almost hard surface thanks to the sesame seeds, which fry up in the oil to a crusty golden brown. Underneath this surface lies a sweet dough made from rice paste that provides excellent textural contrast. In the best of all worlds, fried sesame balls are offered fresh out of the fat so that the dough is thin, hot, and almost creamy.

A marble of red bean paste provides a flavorful bit of interest in each bite. However, this filling is usually outsized by the large bubble of hot air trapped inside as the sweet is fried and the ball expands. The server will almost always snip these open just as they are placed on the table. Exterior is crunchy and then soft and sticky; interior is sweet and pasty.

BASIC FILLING
Smooth red bean paste.

NESTING HABITS
Three fat balls, each with its own paper cup, nestle together on small plates; often available in Chinese bakeries.

ORIGINS
Records of palace sweets from over a thousand years ago show that these were enjoyed in the national capital of Changan (today known as Xi'an of the terra-cotta army) in the desert province of Shaanxi. News of this delicious treat spread far and wide, and it was eventually made a part of the cuisines of the lower Yangtze. However, nowhere did it take hold as well as in Southern China, where cooked, pounded sticky rice is known as 糍粑 · *cíbā* · *ci⁴ baa¹*, a tasty relative of Japanese mochi, and is turned into a wide variety of treats.

SPECIES
- **Fried Sesame Balls with Sesame Paste**
  麻茸煎堆
  máróng jiānduī · *maa⁴ jung⁴ zin¹ deoi¹*
  Sweetened black sesame paste takes the place of the red bean paste, and black sesame seeds might be used as the coating.

SANDY FILLED MOCHI

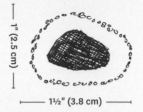

1" (2.5 cm)

1½" (3.8 cm)

GENUS 擂沙湯丸 · *léishā tāngwán* · *leoi⁴ saa¹ tong¹ jyun²*

IDENTIFICATION Soft pillows of steamed rice dough are wrapped around a lavalike filling of ground black sesame seeds, sugar, and fat, and then these are tossed in ground peanuts or soybeans. An ancestor of the famous Japanese versions, sandy filled mochi can be incredibly sensuous with its satiny texture, creamy filling, and crumbly surface. Absolutely at its best when freshly made, as heat then emanates from the dough and makes it melt in the mouth. Exterior is gently gravelly, yielding to a pillowy layer of sticky pounded rice; interior is a semiliquid sweet filling of pulverized sesame seeds and sugar.

BASIC FILLING
Black sesame seeds ground finely and mixed with sugar.

NESTING HABITS
Three fat rice balls are settled in small paper cups on a plate; frequently available in Chinese bakeries.

ORIGINS
These most likely originated a very long time ago (some say during the Song dynasty, 960 to 1279) in the lower Yangtze River Valley, where these are called 湯圓 · *tāngyuán* · *tong¹ jyun⁴* ("soup balls") and are usually served either in sweetened hot water or a hot fermented rice broth; savory ones with meat fillings are also enjoyed there. The most famous center for rice paste creations is in Ningbo, a Zhejiang seaport. Rice paste is popular throughout most of Southern China, and each cuisine has its own particular spin on the sticky rice paste known generally as *ciba* (page 121).

SPECIES
- **Snowy Mango Mochi**
  芒果雪米糍
  mángguǒ xuě mǐcí ·
  mong⁴ gwo² syut³ mai⁵ ci⁴
  Tiny fresh cubes of ripe mango are wrapped inside the mochi, with the outside covered in shredded coconut.

- **Mochi in Syrup**
  糖不甩
  táng bùshuǎi · *tong⁴ bat¹ lat¹*
  Unfilled rice balls are boiled and then tossed over the heat with sugar, ground peanuts, and toasted sesame seeds. The Chinese name means "sugar that can't be shaken off." Served warm.

CHINESE
BEIGNETS

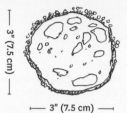

3" (7.5 cm)

3" (7.5 cm)

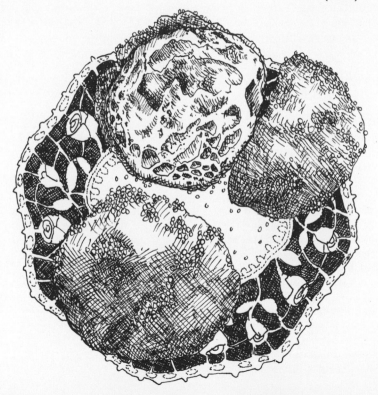

GENUS 白糖沙翁 · *báitáng shāwēng* · *baak⁶ tong⁴ saa¹ jung¹*

IDENTIFICATION Large, craggy fried balls of pastry that taste like eggy raised doughnuts are rolled in white sugar while still hot to give them a sparkly surface. These doughnut holes are very puffy and moist thanks to the large amount of eggs and fat in the batter, which shows that they are very much like their Western cousins, for beignets are also made from a choux dough rich in both ingredients. Their Chinese name means "white sugar sandy old men," probably because the white coating suggests silver hair.

As with just about any deep-fried sweet, these are always at their tastiest when they just emerge from the fat so that the crust is golden and crisp, while the pale interior is hot and custardy. Plain sugar is the main sweet note and seasoning here, and so the coating provides an important contrast for each bite. Exterior is crunchy and sandy; interior is soft and eggy.

NESTING HABITS
Two or three usually show up on paper doilies or in individual paper cups perched on a small plate.

ORIGINS
One theory holds that these most likely started out as fried rice-dough treats. However, another good possibility is that they evolved into a Chinese snack from a very similar Portuguese treat called *malasadas*, since the Portuguese had laid claim to various treaty ports in China and even possessed a coastal colony there in the form of Macau. In the northern province of Henan, these beignets are called "glassy egg balls," and something very similar can be found in both Okinawa and Hawaii, where they are respectively referred to as *sata andagi* and *malasadas*.

SPECIES
Sui generis.

SWEET POTATO POCKETS

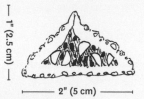

1" (2.5 cm)

2" (5 cm)

GENUS 潮州油粿 · *Cháozhōu yóuguǒ* · *Ciu⁴ zau¹ jau⁴ gwo²*

IDENTIFICATION The combination of sweet potatoes with sticky rice flour places this dish firmly within the realm of classic Chaozhou cooking. Red-fleshed sweet potatoes are peeled, cooked, and mashed before the rice flour is kneaded in.

This slightly tacky wrapper holds another hallmark signature of Chaozhou: a crumbly filling of peanuts, sesame seeds, and crunchy sugar. The wrapper is folded around the filling to form a triangle, the edges are sealed, and then the packet is deep-fried until puffy and golden brown. These are always best when freshly made and still piping hot. Exterior is a slightly crisp surface that quickly yields to a sticky, molten dough tasting of sweet potatoes; interior is sandy, nutty, and sweet.

BASIC FILLING
Chopped toasted peanuts, toasted sesame seeds, and turbinado sugar.

NESTING HABITS
Three golden triangles generally are snuggled into small paper cups or on a paper doily to absorb the oil.

ORIGINS
The main type of rice used is sticky, which gives the dough a wonderful texture the Chinese love that is called "Q" in Taiwanese, or "chewy." Variations on these treats can be savory instead of sweet, or they may contain a combination of sweet with savory. *Guo* (page 82) used to be shaped with wooden molds to give them the form of tortoises or peaches. Traditionally, these steamed sweets were then used as offerings to the deities at celebrations, at funerals, and when asking for divine favors. The filling for such offerings is generally sweetened mung bean paste seasoned with green onions or peanuts.

SPECIES
- **Pumpkin Pockets**
  南瓜餅
  nánguā bǐng · *naam⁴ gwaa¹ beng²*
  Popular in places like Sichuan, pumpkin stands in for the sweet potatoes, and these are often filled with sweet red bean paste or a creamier mixture; may be pan-fried.

FRIED WATER CHESTNUT GELÉE

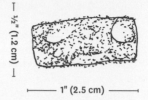

½" (1.2 cm)

1" (2.5 cm)

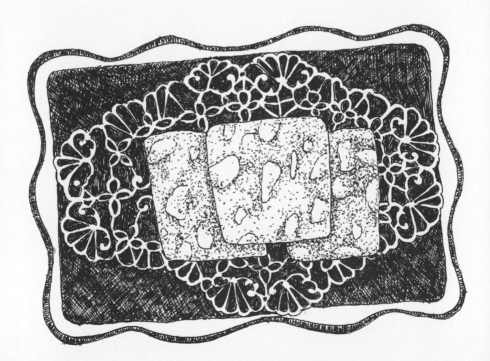

GENUS 油煎馬蹄糕 • *yóujiān mǎtí gāo* • *jau⁴ zin¹ maa⁵ tai⁴ gou¹*

IDENTIFICATION Flat squares that look like sheets of amber contain ivory nuggets of water chestnuts. These squares are pan-fried to form a golden crust on both flat sides. The translucent amber is actually water chestnut flour mixed with water and sugar, and this transforms into a quivering gel once it is steamed.

The water chestnuts suspended in the gelée are incredibly delicious when fresh rather than canned, and these are peeled before being either coarsely chopped, slivered, or simply crushed open. Lightly sweet so that the flavor of the water chestnuts can be fully appreciated, the pudding is sliced and pan-fried prior to serving. Exterior is slightly rough and crispy; interior is jellylike and studded with crunchy bits of water chestnut.

NESTING HABITS
Three slices on a plate, usually nesting on a paper doily.

ORIGINS
Water chestnuts are sweet corms that grow under water. Just as the tomato is actually a fruit but is treated like a vegetable, and rhubarb is a vegetable that usually masquerades as a fruit, the water chestnut tastes as if it should be a fruit, rather than an unusual vegetable. Outside of Southern China, they are called 荸薺 • *bíqì*, and Guangxi is the most renowned producer of this very Chinese ingredient.

SPECIES
• **Deep-Fried Water Chestnut Rolls**
  脆皮馬蹄條
  cuìpí mǎtí tiáo • *ceoi³ pei⁴ maa⁵ tai⁴ tiu⁴*
  Water chestnut gelée is cut into batons and then either coated in batter or rolled up in a spring roll wrapper before being fried.

• **Water Chestnut Gelée**
  馬蹄糕
  mǎtí gāo • *maa⁵ tai⁴ gou¹*
  This delicate sweet is the same as the main genus, except that it is not fried, but simply cut into cubes.

HOT + WARM

129

DURIAN
PUFFS

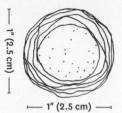

1" (2.5 cm)

1" (2.5 cm)

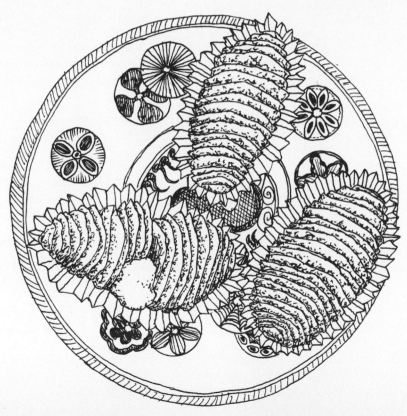

GENUS 榴槤酥 · *líulián sū* · *lau⁴ lin⁴ sou¹*

IDENTIFICATION Ribbed puff pastry fried to a golden brown encases a creamy center that tastes of durian. This Southeast Asia fruit has a bad rap, as it not only looks unfriendly—it's a huge, unwieldly football covered with serious spikes—but also the smell is described by its detractors as decidedly rotten. However, this fruit is also beloved by countless others who find the slightly oniony yet sweet flesh deeply aromatic and so enticing that it comes across as downright seductive.

On the surface, this sweet looks very much like Radish Puffs (page 70), as Southern-style puff pastry is wrapped around in a coil that explodes into corrugated frills. The traditional filling is pure durian flesh, but nowadays most places make do with a pastry cream colored pale yellow and flavored with durian extract, which still can be quite tasty when done right. Sometimes baked instead of deep-fried, these are stellar when freshly cooked, although they manage to retain their delicate crunch as they cool. Exterior is crispy, flaky, and buttery; interior is creamy and imbued with deep tropical flavors.

NESTING HABITS
Three flaky puffs are first cradled in paper cupcake liners before being arranged on a small plate.

ORIGINS
These very probably got their start in the kitchens of Chinese chefs somewhere in Southeast Asia—at least, that is this author's unsubstantiated guess—because the best durian are grown in places like Thailand, where they are regarded as the king of fruit.

Something as strangely delectable as this fruit was bound to be turned into a dessert, and wrapping their flesh in puff pastry shows considerable culinary brilliance, as this allows the powerful aromas to be enjoyed in gentle whiffs, while the smooth texture is given the perfect counterpoint in the flaky crust.

SPECIES
Sui generis.

DEEP-FRIED MILK

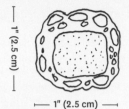

1" (2.5 cm)

1" (2.5 cm)

GENUS 脆皮鲜奶 · *cuìpí xiānnǎi* · *ceoi³ pei⁴ sin¹ naai⁵*

IDENTIFICATION A creamy center of white custard is surrounded here by a crispy fried exterior. Milk (usually evaporated) is simmered together with sugar, egg whites, and either corn or potato starch to form a thick paste that is then poured into a pan and cooled. The chilled pudding is cut into batons and dipped in a light batter that forms an airy, crispy coating once it is deep-fried.

This is best special ordered so that it can be enjoyed fresh out of the fat. Sometimes sprinkled with sugar before serving. Exterior is a crunchy batter with mild flavors; interior is a molten white custard that is lightly sweet. The main genus therefore sports a name that means "crispy-skinned milk," but it is also known in Chinese as 炸鲜奶 · *zhá xiānnǎi* · *zaa³ sin¹ naai⁵,* or simply "deep-fried milk."

BASIC FILLING
Pale sweet custard made from egg whites, sugar, milk, and starch.

NESTING HABITS
Three or so thick batons stacked atop a paper doily.

ORIGINS
The rich Pearl River Delta that covers the huge swath of land south of Guangzhou is home to China's ancient mulberry orchards. These trees produced the leaves that fed the silkworms that created the fabric that the whole of the rest of the world has coveted ever since the heydays of the Roman Empire. Cattle have also historically been raised here primarily for their milk, which has traditionally not been enjoyed fresh, but rather turned into local specialties that cook the milk and so kill the enzyme that causes indigestion for many Chinese. Hot congealed sweets like double-skinned milk and ginger pudding are famous here, as are dishes like stir-fried milk, a savory concoction that features seafood and nuts.

SPECIES
- **Custard Spring Rolls**
  奶皇春捲
  nǎihuáng chūnjuǎn · *naai⁵ wong⁴ ceon¹ gyun²*
  A yellow custard much like the filling in Custard Tarts (page 160) is wrapped in spring roll wrappers and deep-fried.

TAPIOCA
PUDDING

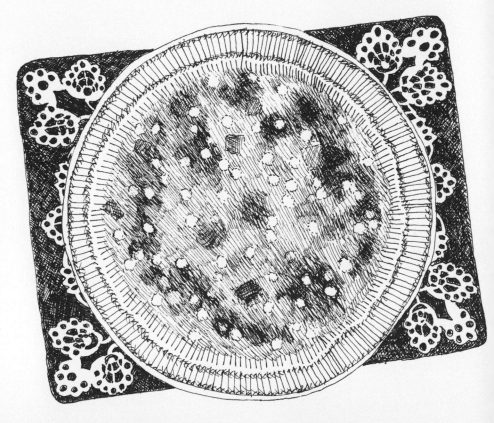

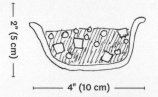

2" (5 cm)

4" (10 cm)

GENUS 西米布丁 · *xīmǐ bùdīng* · *sai¹ mai⁵ bou³ ding¹*

IDENTIFICATION Tiny round balls of tapioca are suspended in a pudding thickened with eggs and usually filled with taro or sweet red beans and coconut milk. Almost always offered in a small casserole, this is a baked dish that should have leopard spots on the top from being browned under a broiler.

Exterior is chewy and firm; interior is soft and molten with small pieces of powdery taro or creamy beans. In Cantonese, this pudding is generally referred to as 西米布甸 · *xīmǐ bùdlàn* · *sai¹ mai⁵ bou³ din⁶*, which is simply another way of saying "tapioca pudding."

BASIC FILLING
Coconut or evaporated milk, sugar, eggs, small tapioca pearls, and either red beans or taro.

NESTING HABITS
A single small casserole perched on a doily and settled on a plate; despite its size, it is meant to be shared.

ORIGINS
Baked egg-based puddings were most definitely introduced to China by the British in Guangzhou. But like all the great dishes in that part of the country, the local chefs took that basic template and transformed it into something indisputably Chinese. Coconut milk sometimes takes the place of dairy, round pearls of tapioca provide the smooth chewy texture so different from Western tapioca, sweet red beans may dot the interior, and the lavender batons of taro ground the dessert with a comforting sweetness and starchy texture. The pearls used in this dish can be made from either actual tapioca or sago, as they are considered interchangeable.

SPECIES
- **Chilled Coconut Tapioca Pudding** 冰凍椰汁西米布丁
  bīngdòng yézhī xīmǐ bùdīng · *bing¹ dong³ je⁴ zap¹ sai¹ mai⁵ bou³ ding¹*
  Very similar to Coconut Milk Jellies (page 151), this pudding includes a healthy handful of tapioca pearls to lighten the mixture and add beautiful texture.

LOTUS SEED
PASTE BUNS

GENUS 蓮蓉包 · *liánróng bāo* · *lin⁴ jung⁴ baau¹*

IDENTIFICATION Fluffy, plain yeast bread dough very similar to what is used with savory buns—such as Vegetarian Buns (page 24)—is wrapped around a sweet, pasty filling, sealed with a topknot or turned over for a smooth surface, and then steamed. An almost even balance of bread to sweet paste is aimed for here to provide textural balance, as well as to offer contrasts in flavor with each bite.

The bread should have enough gluten so that it does not stick to the teeth, which is why pastry flour is not used in better-quality buns, and a slow rising gives the dough a deep, yeasty flavor. Inside the buns is a thick beige paste consisting of finely mashed lotus seeds mixed with fat and sugar. These seeds have a delicate fragrance that marries well with the bread; lesser quality fillings will use mashed white beans instead of the lotus seeds. Has a small square of waxed paper on the bottom. Exterior is fluffy with a smooth surface; interior is pasty, sweet, and slightly buttery.

BASIC FILLING
Finely mashed lotus seeds, sugar, and fat.

NESTING HABITS
Two or three buns in a steamer or on a plate; often sighted in Chinese bakeries.

ORIGINS
As with all steamed buns, these originated in the North, and Shandong is still famed for its wide variety of steamed breads. Lotus seed paste most likely was born in the Yangtze River Valley, where lotus plants grow rampantly in the warm climate and plentiful bodies of still water. However, lotus paste is probably most popular in the Guangdong area, where it is a beloved filling for a wide variety of pastries and other sweets.

SPECIES
- **Sesame Seed Paste Buns**
  芝麻包
  zhīmá bāo · *zi¹ mau⁴ baau¹*
  Identical to the main genus, but with finely ground black sesame paste packed inside.

- **Red Bean Paste Buns**
  豆沙包
  dòushā bāo · *dau⁶ saa¹ baau¹*
  Sweet red bean paste takes the place of the lotus seed paste.

CUSTARD
BUNS

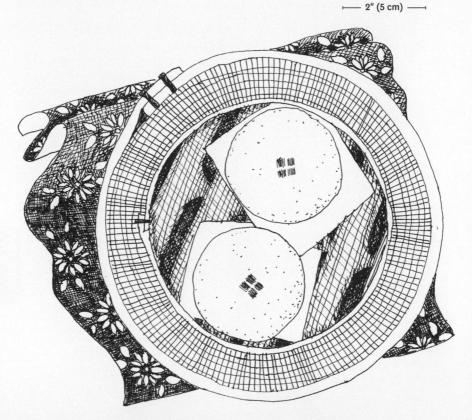

2" (5 cm)

2" (5 cm)

GENUS 奶黃包 · *nǎihuáng bāo* · *naai⁵ wong⁴ baau¹*

IDENTIFICATION Smooth raised wheat dough encloses a rich paste with sweet-and-salty flavors. The white dough provides a stark contrast to the brilliant yellow of the crumbly filling. Each teahouse and bakery seems to have a different way of making these steamed delights, but inevitably the center should be a slightly grainy thick custard seasoned with mashed brined egg yolks. Oftentimes the top of the bun is marked with red dots to signify the filling, as steamed buns tend to all look alike until they are opened.

The springy wrapper should be chewy enough that it contrasts nicely with the creamy center, but these are always best when hot so that the bread remains tender while the filling turns molten and even more satisfying. Has a small square of waxed paper on the bottom. Exterior is smooth and springy; interior is custardy and slightly sandy.

BASIC FILLING
Milk, butter, eggs, flour, cornstarch, finely mashed brined egg yolks, and custard powder or Parmesan cheese.

NESTING HABITS
Two or three buns in a steamer or on a plate; often available in Chinese bakeries.

ORIGINS
The British are probably responsible for the initial inspiration for the filling, for custard is a Western import. However, local chefs made these buns uniquely Chinese with the inspired incorporation of savory brined yolks, and in the process amping up that mild custard with a delicious range of flavors and textures. These most likely developed in Guangzhou as breakfast or snack offerings, as they are splendid with a cup of hot, strong tea.

SPECIES
- **Lava Custard Buns**
  流沙奶皇包
  liúshā nǎihuáng bāo ·
  lau⁴ saa¹ naai⁵ wong⁴ baau¹
  Very similar to the main genus, lava custard buns differ only in that the filling is very loose and creamy. When hot enough, the custard will squirt satisfyingly on the tongue, a delicious mixture of tasty pleasure and painful heat.

SNOW-TOPPED BUNS

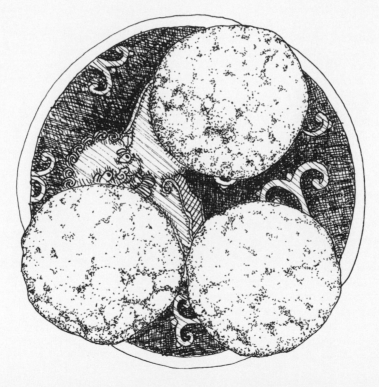

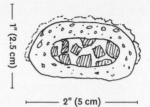

1" (2.5 cm)

2" (5 cm)

GENUS 雪山包 · *xuěshān bāo* · *syut³ saan¹ baau¹*

IDENTIFICATION Round, fat baked buns made with a gently sweet egg dough contain a filling that is always sweet to a certain degree. They get their name from the white, flaky, crisp layer that covers the smooth top of the bun. Developed in relatively recent times mainly as an afternoon snack rather than as part of the traditional dim sum experience, snow-topped buns are becoming increasingly popular throughout Chinese metropolitan areas. The center can be made out of something like *char siu* and mixed with seasonings like soy sauce and hoisin sauce, but the more common dessert fillings tend to be creamy and silky, although regular sweet pastes like red bean and lotus seed sometimes appear, as well.

Exterior is craggy and crumbly on top, yielding to a smooth baked yeast dough that is slightly sweet like a Parker House roll; interior varies, but generally is sweet and more or less smooth.

BASIC FILLING
Creamy taro, red bean paste, custard, lotus seed paste, or something similar.

NESTING HABITS
Three or so nestled together on a plate; often available in Chinese bakeries.

ORIGINS
Snow-topped buns are new members of the dim sum family and appear to be Hong Kong variants on the pineapple buns so popular in Hong Kong and Taiwan. Those pineapple buns, in turn, probably developed out of the very

similar sunrise buns of Japan, which are in turn variations on Mexican *concha* buns. It's a small world, after all.

SPECIES
• **Pineapple Buns**
  菠蘿麵包
  bōluó miànbāo · *bo¹ lo⁴ min⁶ baau¹*
  Generally found in bakeries rather than dim sum houses, these buns get their name from the diamond-shaped patterns on the yellow coating, and they usually have no filling.

FIGURATIVE BUNS

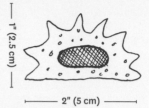

1" (2.5 cm)

2" (5 cm)

GENUS 象形包子 · *xiàngxíng bāozi* · *zoeng⁶ jing⁴ baau¹ zi²*

IDENTIFICATION Tensile white steamed bread dough is wrapped around some sort of filling and then fashioned into a whole animal, animal head, mushroom, vegetable, or fruit. This is done by either shaping the bread with the hands or cutting the dough with scissors. The dough is at times colored for contrasting details, and the eyes of animals are always marked.

Traditionally, these buns depict rabbits or hedgehogs, but in recent years the love for cartoon-type characters has taken over the field, leading to buns shaped like the heads of pandas, pigs, and even Hello Kitty. Like all steamed buns, these relatively new dim sum offerings have small waxed paper squares on the bottom to keep them from sticking to the steamer. Exterior is smooth, dry, and sometimes knobby yielding to a tensile steamed bread dough; interior is smooth or mildly chunky, but always flavorful.

BASIC FILLING
Sweetened red bean, lotus seed, red date, or taro paste; savory buns may contain seasoned mushroom, meat, or seafood fillings.

NESTING HABITS
Three huddled together on a plate; often found clustered in Chinese bakery display cases.

ORIGINS
Figurative buns probably were the brainchild of some creative chefs somewhere up the line who wanted to spiff up the banquet table, but no one knows for sure where or when.

As sweet steamed buns started a long time ago up in Shandong province, these might even be Northern inventions. Some chefs color the dough orange and create pumpkin shapes to hold pumpkin filling or make ears of corn to suggest the creamy corn centers, but generally the shape has nothing to do with what is inside (for what would panda or Hello Kitty buns be hiding?), as these are more about being fanciful and fun than anything else.

SPECIES
Sui generis.

MANGO
PUDDING

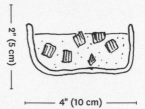

2" (5 cm)

4" (10 cm)

GENUS 芒果布丁 · *mángguǒ bùdīng* · *mong⁴ gwo² bou³ ding¹*

IDENTIFICATION This smooth, apricot-colored pudding is often studded with bits of ripe orange-hued mango to both emphasize the tropical flavors and provide visual and textural delight. Mango pudding can sometimes appear in a bowl or clear plastic cup, but more often than not, enough gelatin or agar is added to the mixture so that it can be turned out into little molded servings. Sweetened condensed milk is mixed with mango puree to make this pudding, and it provides just the right note of buttery creaminess and sweetness against the rich, tart-edged fruit.

When served in a cup or bowl, the texture can sometimes approach the sublime, as just enough thickener is then used to result in a trembling, quivering balance between solid and liquid. Exterior and interior are the same: smooth, chilled pudding with a creamy texture, sometimes with small chunks of mango inside. In Cantonese, this is usually referred to as 芒果布甸 · *mángguǒ bùdiàn* · *mong⁴ gwo² bou³ din⁶*, which also means "mango pudding."

NESTING HABITS
One bowl or cup presented on top of a doily-covered plate, or a number of smallish unmolded puddings arrayed on a plate; often found hovering in the refrigerated cases at Chinese bakeries.

ORIGINS
Unlike many of China's chilled puddings, this one did not originate in England, but rather was most likely introduced to Guangzhou from India by the British. The North Indian dessert called *mango phirni* is very similar to mango pudding in that finely pureed fruit pulp is cooked with milk, sugar, and rice flour to form a thickened mixture that is then chilled. Gelatin and agar have taken the place of the rice flour here, but everything else has remained pretty much the same.

SPECIES
• **Durian Pudding**
榴槤布丁
líulián bùdīng · *lau⁴ lin⁴ bou³ ding¹*
Pureed durian takes the place of the mango in this dish, and so it generally is completely smooth.

SOY PUDDING

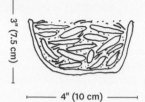

3" (7.5 cm)

4" (10 cm)

GENUS 豆腐花 · *dòufǔhuā* · *dau⁶ fu⁶ faa¹*

IDENTIFICATION Silky lobes of super tender *doufu* (that is, bean curd or tofu) are scooped out of a wooden bucket or large pot into an individual bowl. Little more than rich soy milk that has been clabbered with food-grade plaster, this has the mouthfeel of the finest pudding. A caramelized amber or clear sugar syrup flavored with shreds of fresh ginger is then ladled over the top, sometimes with peeled boiled peanuts added as a delicious fillip.

Unlike other similar sweets, soy pudding is not molded in a bowl. Instead, a small amount of powdered plaster is mixed into a large container of hot, fresh soy milk, and this starts the clabbering process, much like cheese. The genius touch here is the ladling of the pudding into thin layers: this allows the syrup to mingle with the pudding and offer luscious contrasts with each bite. Exterior and interior are soft and silky with a smooth, ginger-flecked syrup. Sometimes referred to in Chinese and English as simply 豆花 · *dòuhuā* · *dau⁶ faa¹* ("bean flowers").

NESTING HABITS
Layers of plain pudding burrow down in the bowl and are bathed with a ginger syrup; this can be either an individual serving or group dish, depending upon the size.

ORIGINS
Soy milk, bean curd, and all of their relations evolved in Northern China. Shandong province is still considered the home of some of China's best soy milk, and this pudding is jelled up in the North using brine instead of plaster. Since dairy products really never took hold in China outside a few areas in the west and near Guangzhou (page 133), the country's main ethnic group—the Han Chinese—have turned to soy milk, which has fed the imaginations of Chinese chefs and the stomachs of billions of Chinese for countless centuries.

SPECIES
- **Red Bean Soy Pudding**
  紅豆豆腐花
  hóngdòu dòufǔhuā ·
  hung⁴ dau² dau⁶ fu⁶ faa¹
  Identical to the main genus, except that sweetened, boiled red beans are sprinkled over the top, sometimes with a bit of syrup.

GUILING
JELLY

4" (10 cm)

4" (10 cm)

GENUS 龜苓膏 · *guīlíng gāo* · *gwai¹ ling⁴ gou¹*

IDENTIFICATION This is definitely one of the more unusual dishes you will find on a dim sum sweets cart. A large number of Chinese therapeutic herbs give this jelly its deep, almost black color and herbal flavors. It is traditionally made with the bottom plate of the golden shell turtle, but nowadays this expensive and rare ingredient is usually skipped in favor of more herbs, which sometimes may include ginseng, but which always centers on flowers like honeysuckle and chrysanthemum combined with the strongly flavored roots of *Rehmannia* and the fruits of forsythia and a pealike plant called *Abrus*.

According to Chinese medicine, guiling jelly is considered an all-around tonic that is especially refreshing in summer. Usually gently sweetened with honey or sugar, the natural underlying taste is slightly bitter. It has thickening agents like cornstarch mixed in to give it a nice, wobbly texture, and the jelly is often cut up into small cubes and then drizzled with a light syrup, sweetened condensed milk, or milk and honey to mellow out its inherent flavors. Exterior is creamy, sweet, and cool; interior is bouncy, cool, and herbal with a mild bitterness.

NESTING HABITS
A solid cup of jelly or a tumble of dark cubes is drizzled with syrup or condensed milk.

ORIGINS
Guiling jelly is a specialty of Guangxi and Guangdong. Only the bottom plate of one specific type of turtle is traditionally used in Chinese medicine because it is soft enough for its calcium to dissolve during the slow cooking process. During that time, the essences of herbal medicines are also allowed to seep out into the liquid and lend their color, aroma, and medical properties to the tincture.

SPECIES
- **Grass Jelly**
  仙草凍
  xiāncǎo dòng · *sin¹ cou⁹ dung³*
  Very similar in color and texture to guiling jelly, this is made with one herb only—a member of the mint family called *Mesona chinensis*—that turns the unsweetened brew into a gel. This is cubed and tossed with a syrup, added to *boba* (aka pearl) tapioca drinks, or used to garnish shaved ice.

DATE PASTE JELLIES

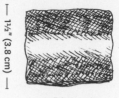

Ⓥ

1½" (3.8 cm)

1½" (3.8 cm)

GENUS 棗皇糕 · *zǎohuáng gāo* · *zou² wong⁴ gou¹*

IDENTIFICATION Shimmering diamonds with alternating layers of deep mulberry hues set against either dusky pink or white, these jellies are meant to be savored with a cup of good tea either as an afternoon snack or at the end of a filling meal.

Dried red dates are poached in nothing but water, and then this highly flavorful juice is mixed with sugar and regular rice flour (and sometimes sweet potato flour) to form the wine-colored layers, while the lighter ones are left unflavored or gently tinted with the date juice. This is then steamed and chilled before being cut into diamonds or squares. Exterior and interior are gently chewy and sticky, and this becomes soft and luscious in the mouth.

NESTING HABITS
Three or four diamonds or squares cut from a sheet cluster together on a plate.

ORIGINS
Many of the Chinese references to this sweet include place-names like Xinjiang or Shanxi, which suggest that this was developed west on the Silk Road somewhere. But what those places are actually referring to is the origin of the red dates (or "jujubes") that supply the flavor and color to this dish. Date paste jellies most likely were developed out of the sweets once served to royalty behind the walls of the Forbidden Palace in Beijing.

SPECIES
- **Wolfberry Jellies**
  枸杞糕
  gǒuqǐ gāo · *gau² gei² gou¹*
  Wolfberries (aka *gouqi* or goji berries) are suspended in a clear amber jelly, often with speckles of water chestnuts or osmanthus blossoms, and sometimes flavored with chrysanthemum flowers.

- **Coconut Milk Jellies**
  椰汁糕
  yézhī gāo · *je⁴ zap¹ gou¹*
  Sweetened coconut milk is thickened with gelatin or cornstarch, making this very similar to Hawaiian haupia.

RED BEAN TAPIOCA BALLS

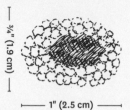

¾" (1.9 cm)

1" (2.5 cm)

GENUS 紅豆西米糕 · *hóngdòu xīmǐ gāo* · *hung⁴ dau² sai¹ mai⁵ gou¹*

IDENTIFICATION The nubby, translucent surface of these sweets reveals a dark center filled with pureed sweetened red beans. Tiny pearls of Asian tapioca are cooked until they are soft but still retain their chewy mouthfeel, and then they are mixed with a touch of sugar and some gelatin to both season and hold them together. They can be rolled into balls or even molded into hearts or other shapes, but the center always has that delectable contrasting filling.

Unusual and yet utterly entrancing, these sweets are generally tacky enough on the surface to withstand being picked up with either chopsticks or fingers, although they are often nestled inside small paper cups to help keep them from jumbling together into a chaotic heap. Part of the allure—especially of the ones that are simply rolled into balls—lies in the overall bumpiness of the surface, as this sets it apart from all other Chinese sweets and provides the most marvelous texture for the lips and tongue to explore. Exterior is tacky and adorably lumpy; interior is sweet and pasty.

BASIC FILLING
Mashed cooked red beans sweetened with sugar.

NESTING HABITS
Three or four resting in little paper cups and gathered on a small plate.

ORIGINS
Most of China's tapioca-based sweets appear to have developed in Guangzhou or thereabouts. Sago pearl desserts are common in India, so it is possible that they were either introduced to Southern China by the British, or else they traveled first to Southeast Asia and then up the tropical coast into Guangzhou and Hainan island.

SPECIES
- **Taro Tapioca Sweets**
  香芋西米糕
  xiāngyù xīmǐ gāo · *hoeng¹ wu⁶ sai¹ mai⁵ gou¹*
  Finely pureed cooked taro is added to the tapioca, and so there usually is no need for a filling.

SESAME
ROLLUPS

(V)

1" (2.5 cm)

1" (2.5 cm)

GENUS 芝麻卷 · *zhīmá juǎn* · *zi¹ maa⁴ gyun²*

IDENTIFICATION Long, translucent layers of black paste are rolled up like carpets in this attractive and delicious sweet. Finely ground sesame seeds are mixed with water chestnut and rice flours, sugar, and water to form a thin slurry. This is spread into an extremely thin layer on a pan, steamed until set, and rolled up into a tight cylinder before being chilled and cut into 4-inch (10-cm) lengths.

These teahouse favorites have such a distinctive appearance that they sometimes get called "rolls of film" (菲林卷 · *fēilín juǎn* · *fei¹ lam⁴ gyun²*) in Cantonese. The water chestnut flour gives these sweets a lovely bounce and the consistency of a gummy bear left out in the sun. Diners can unroll them for a completely different texture, turning them into fine, silky sheets that melt on the tongue. Inky black and lightly nutty, these are the perfect way to end a heavy meal. Exterior and interior are tacky, springy, and gently chewy. Sometimes called 黑芝麻卷 · *hēi zhīmá juǎn* · *hak¹ zi¹ maa⁴ gyun²* ("black sesame rollups").

NESTING HABITS
Four pieces nestled up against each other on a small plate.

ORIGINS
A relatively new member of the dim sum family, this sweet began appearing in Hong Kong teahouses in the 1970s or '80s. It is uncertain who first made these distinctive rollups, but anyone who has ever enjoyed a hot bowl of black sesame soup will recognize what gave that cook such an excellent idea: These soups are made from little more than ground sesame, sugar, and rice flour, and a skin forms on the surface as it cools.

Someone probably played around with this idea, adding water chestnut flour and searching for the right ratios until, voilà, a dessert was born.

SPECIES
- **Haw Rollups**
  山楂卷
  shānzhā juǎn · *saan¹ caa⁴ gyun²*
  This reddish Northern treat is more like a Western fruit leather, as it is simply finely ground haw fruits mixed with sugar, dried in thin sheets, and rolled up. It is a sweet treat popular only in the colder areas of China.

RAISED
FERMENTED
RICE CAKE

3/4" (1.9 cm)

3" (7.5 cm)

GENUS 倫教糕 · *Lúnjiào gāo* · *Leon⁴ gaau³ gou¹*

IDENTIFICATION These thin, pie-shaped wedges or diamonds of a spongy white cake possess the wonderful aroma and taste of fermented rice. Plain white rice is soaked and then ground to a fine slurry before sugar water and levain (a starter that contains wild yeast) are added; much like in traditional breadmaking, the levain is simply a bit of the previous fermented batch and is used here instead of wine or bread yeast, as it provides the leavening and the mature winey aromas that make this sweet so distinctive. The batter is then allowed to slowly rise and ferment a bit (but not so long that it turns sour), and then it is poured into cake pans and steamed. The result is a pure white, very bouncy cake with a shiny surface and long vertical bubbles inside.

These are best chilled, which dampens the stickiness a bit and emphasizes the lovely aromas of rice wine. Exterior is tacky and very smooth; interior is gently sweet and very aromatic, as well as ribboned with long vertical bubbles that dance on the tongue. Often referred to as 白糖糕 · *háitáng gāo* · *baak⁶ tong⁴ gou¹* ("white sugar cake") in Cantonese.

NESTING HABITS
In teahouses, these may appear as a single wedge or a cluster of three or four diamonds on a plate, while in Chinese bakeries these are almost always served as wedges.

ORIGINS
A sweets maker in the Pearl River Delta is credited with this creation, and it is named after his village near the city of Shunde: Lunjiao. Legend has it that this occurred back during the Ming dynasty (1368 to 1644), when that cook named Liang made what he thought was a bad batch of layered rice cake, but it actually turned out to be even tastier than the original.

SPECIES
- **Layered Rice Sponge Cake**
  鬆糕
  sōnggāo · *sung¹ gou¹*
  A sweetened batter of ground plain rice and sticky rice sandwiches a layer of sweet red bean paste, and this is steamed to form a dense cake, usually topped with preserved fruits and sold in bakeries in the autumn.

MALAY CAKE

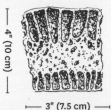

4" (10 cm)

3" (7.5 cm)

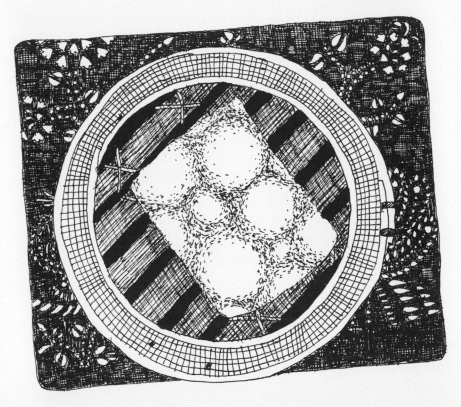

GENUS 馬拉糕 · *Mǎlā gāo* · *Maa⁵ laai¹ gou¹*

IDENTIFICATION A light steamed sponge cake cut into large squares or wedges and served in steamer baskets. Generally a pale golden brown, Malay cake gets its unique color and subtly savory edge from soy sauce that is added to the eggy batter. A staple of teahouse dessert carts, this ideally is a plain, unfrosted cake filled with millions of tiny bubbles, with the occasional large bubbles near the top. Those made in the traditional way with a slow levain-induced rising will have three distinct layers, while cakes made with baking powder will have a more uniform sponge.

Teahouses generally have a single large cake in the kitchen that is sliced into serving sizes, and each piece gets its own small basket, which allows it to be heated through on the carts. Exterior is tacky and shiny; interior is very spongy, mildly sweet, and light.

NESTING HABITS
One to six pieces are presented in a steamer basket lined with paper; often available in Chinese bakeries.

ORIGINS
This is a Hong Kong sweet that might have been developed from a Singapore recipe, which in turn seems to be a riff on an English sponge cake. All of this makes sense once you realize that both Singapore and Hong Kong were once British colonies, and many of the United Kingdom's ways with food evolved as they were absorbed into the local cuisines.

SPECIES
• **Black Sugar Cake**
  黑糖糕
  hēitáng gāo · *hak¹ tong⁴ gou¹*
  Very dark brown sugar flavors this simple steamed sponge cake made with rice and wheat flours.

• **Egg Yolk Thousand Layer Cake**
  蛋黃千層糕
  dànhuáng qiāncéng gāo ·
  daan² wong⁴ cin¹ cang⁴ gou¹
  Layers of sweet, milky sponge cake sandwich a rich filling of such things as shredded coconut, sugar, and brined egg yolks, and the confection is then steamed. These are generally only seven layers high, but who's counting?

CAKES +
TARTS

CUSTARD TARTS

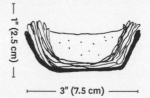

1" (2.5 cm)

3" (7.5 cm)

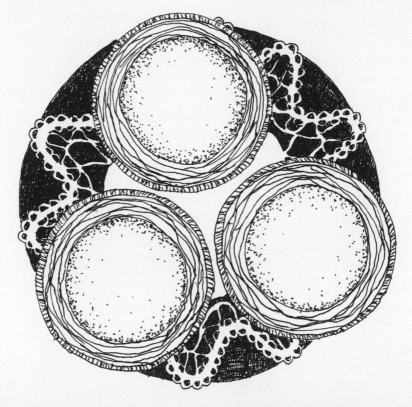

GENUS 蛋撻 · *dàntà* · *daan² taat³*

IDENTIFICATION Tartlets of Chinese puff or short pastry hold puddles of sweet, quivery custard. Terrific when freshly made and still a bit hot, these tarts can also be enjoyed warm or cool, and each one usually serves a single diner, although you can ask that they be cut in half. The top surface ought to be as shiny as a mirror, and the custard should be a deep lemon yellow with the faint aroma of vanilla. Exterior is crisp and flaky; interior is soft, gently sweet, and eggy.

BASIC FILLING
Eggs, milk, sugar, and vanilla.

NESTING HABITS
Three hovering together in small foil cups on a plate; often available in Chinese bakeries.

ORIGINS
Custard tarts are, in all likelihood, a Guangzhou interpretation of the English custard pie as small, open-faced tartlets. Others insist that these are interpretations of *pastéis de nata*, but as Guangzhou and Hong Kong have traditionally served unbrowned custard pies, and since these have been part of British cuisine for at least seven hundred years, custard tarts most probably are direct descendants of the same sweets once enjoyed by Henry the Eighth. They became popular in Guangzhou during the 1920s, when department stores hired chefs to cook special treats like these to lure in customers from their competitors.

SPECIES
- **Portuguese Custard Tarts**
  葡式蛋撻
  Púshì dàntà · *Pou⁴ sik¹ daan² taat³*
  A Macau variation, this tart is based on the *pastel de nata*, as the enclave was a Portuguese colony until only recently. These variations have browned tops, but otherwise are pretty much the same as regular custard tarts.

- **Milk Tarts**
  鮮奶撻
  xiānnǎi tà · *sin¹ naai⁵ taat³*
  These mildly flavored tarts use only the egg whites in the custard, which gives the filling a snowy color.

ACKNOWLEDGMENTS

In only a few short years, *Lucky Peach* has turned into the most amazing biosphere for food writers and artists to blossom. I was therefore incredibly fortunate to have the first incarnation of this book, "The Beginner's Field Guide to Dim Sum," appear in the pages of its fifth issue: "Chinatown" (November 2012). My endless thanks go out to editor-in-chief Chris Ying for taking this project under his generous wing, as well as to everyone else connected with *Lucky Peach*, particularly David Chang, Peter Meehan, Rachel Khong, and Walter Green. The *Lucky Peach* team later fashioned the article into a gorgeous handout for the 2013 MAD Symposium in Copenhagen, designed a DIY download that readers could fold into their very own little field guides, and revived the article yet once again on the *Lucky Peach* website in February 2015. I will always be grateful.

Ten Speed Press has turned into an absolute treasure trove of amazing people. My editor, Emily Timberlake, is a dream to work with and too talented to be believed. Betsy Stromberg is my ideal art director: smart, ingenious, and incredibly gifted. Others at Ten Speed who deserve a deeply grateful shout out include publisher Aaron Wehner for hearing my proposal and saying simply, "Sounds cool," as well as VP Hannah Rahill, senior director of marketing Michele Crim, director of publicity David Hawk, associate marketing and publicity manager Daniel Wikey, and marketing associate Ashley Matuszak. Thanks also to Elisabeth Beller, Karen Levy, and Ken Della Penta.

To the countless dim sum restaurants here and in the Far East who have educated my palate, my humble appreciation for a delicious education. Finally, as always, my thanks to my husband, J. H. Huang, for being my constant companion at the dining table and in life.

ABOUT THE AUTHOR

Jennifer Graham

CAROLYN PHILLIPS is a food writer, scholar, and artist. She is the author of *All Under Heaven: Recipes from the 35 Cuisines of China*. Her work has appeared in such places as *Best Food Writing 2015*, *Lucky Peach*, *Gastronomica*, *Buzzfeed*, *Zester Daily*, *Alimentum*, *Huffington Post*, *Food52*, and at the 2013 MAD Symposium in Copenhagen. She and her husband were cultural consultants on the third *Ghostbusters* movie, her weekly blog is Madame Huang's Kitchen (MadameHuang.com), and she tweets as @madamehuang.

Carolyn's art has appeared everywhere from museums and galleries to various magazines and journals to Nickelodeon's *Supah Ninjas* series. She worked for over a decade as a professional Mandarin interpreter in the federal and state courts, lived in Taiwan for eight years, translated countless books and articles, and married into a Chinese family more than thirty years ago.

INDEX

F

G

Green Onion and Ginger Lo Mein, 111

H

J

L

M

All rights reserved.
Published in the United States by Ten Speed Press, an imprint of the Crown
Publishing Group, a division of Penguin Random House LLC, New York.
www.crownpublishing.com
www.tenspeed.com

Ten Speed Press and the Ten Speed Press colophon are registered trademarks of
Penguin Random House LLC.

Library of Congress Cataloging-in-Publication Data

Names: Phillips, Carolyn J., author.
Title: The dim sum field guide : a taxonomy of dumplings, buns, meats, sweets,
    and other specialties of the Chinese teahouse / written and illustrated by
    Carolyn Phillips.
Description: First edition. | Berkeley : Ten Speed Press, [2016] | Includes
    bibliographical references and index.
Identifiers: LCCN 2015036911
Subjects: LCSH: Dim sum. | Cooking, Chinese—Cantonese style.
Classification: LCC TX724.5.C5 P487 2016 | DDC 641.5951—dc23 LC record
    available at https://lccn.loc.gov/2015036911

Hardcover ISBN: 978-1-60774-956-1
eBook ISBN: 978-1-60774-957-8

Printed in China

Design by Betsy Stromberg

10 9 8 7 6 5 4 3 2 1

First Edition